GARLAND STUDIES IN

# Entrepreneurship

STUART BRUCHEY

University of Maine

GENERAL EDITOR

A Garland Series

# Everybody's Business

Winning the Workforce
2000 Challenge

*June Webb-Vignery*
*M. Elizabeth Lynch*

Garland Publishing, Inc.
New York & London
1992

**Library of Congress Cataloging-in-Publication Data**

Webb-Vignery, June.
    Everybody's business : winning the workforce 2000 challenge / June
Webb-Vignery and M. Elizabeth Lynch.
        p.   cm. — (Garland studies in entrepreneurship)
    ISBN 0-8153-0995-3 (alk. paper)
    1. Working class—United States—Forecasting.  2. Employment forecasting—United
States.  3. Organizational change—United States—Forecasting.  I. Lynch, M.
Elizabeth.  II. Title.  III. Series.
HD8072.5.W43   1992
331.1'0973—dc20                            92-28660
                                                  CIP

Printed on acid-free, 250-year-life paper

Manufactured in the United States of America

DEDICATION

To Bob With Love

June Webb-Vignery

To my mother, Elizabeth M. Lynch, and my deceased father, Ulice C. Lynch, both of whom led by example with strength, courage, a sense of fairness, and a love of God. These values are the foundation for all my paradigms and I feel especially blessed.

M. Elizabeth Lynch

# ACKNOWLEDGMENTS

Sarah Weddington of "Roe v. Wade" fame was finishing her presentation on leadership for the 1990 YWCA Women on the Move Conference in Tucson, Arizona. Questions flowed from the audience as Weddington addressed the problems women and persons of color encounter in today's organizations. She regaled the audience with graphic stories of failed attempts by organizations to effectively address Workforce 2000 issues, and nervous laughter rippled across the room as Weddington described the "glass ceiling" encountered by those historically barred from organizational leadership. Referring to these individuals as "birds in a cage" with their talents and creativity stifled, she said that organizations were going to have to "wake up" if they were to survive in the 21st century.

We would like to thank Ms. Weddington for inspiring the questions that led to this book on the need for a new organizational paradigm that incorporates people and knowledge presently rejected by organizations. Some of those questions are: 1. What is the old paradigm mindset governing many organizations today that inhibits the addressing of Workforce 2000 issues, and why are many of the best and most creative individuals leaving these organizations simply because they do not fit?; 2. Why are dysfunctional organizations especially at risk in addressing workforce changes needed for the 21st century?; and 3. How can organizations shift to a new paradigm which fully incorporates Workforce 2000 participants?

It is our contention that organizations can and must adjust to changes in American society which threaten the organization's very survival. Changes ranging from demographic shifts within the workforce to an accelerating technological imperative challenge today's antiquated organizational human resource systems. Although these systems contain elements that could contribute to organizational change, they are generally ineffective and reflect the past rather than the future. To deal with the challenges of Workforce 2000, employers need to shift to a new paradigm and remove the mental and communication obstacles now precluding change. This change is "Everybody's Business."

Several persons have helped to make this book possible. It is a pleasure to thank them and also to absolve them of any inadequacies that remain despite our best efforts. Particular thanks to David Lawrence, editor and publisher of *The Miami Herald*, who not only accepted our phone call, but invited us to meet with him to discuss an issue he feels very strongly about. His insights and practical experience on the leadership role in the change process were invaluable. As we were writing this book we considered many titles. It was during an Executive Women's Council Christmas party that Roggie Edberg suggested the title we finally chose, *Everybody's Business*. We are indebted to attorney Richard Martinez, Mort Grayam and Marilyn Steffel of Walgreens Company for graciously allowing us to interview them and for their discussions of issues and programs that work in today's organizations. Thank you to Hildegard Steinbach, whose hard work transformed rough drafts into final copy. Also to Bob Vignery, who edited and gave advice on how to say what we really wanted to say and who helped us crystallize our conception of the organizational myth.

Exercising our authors' prerogatives, each of us would like to recognize personal relationships that have helped to shape our lives and our views of the world within which we live.

June: To my sons Mark and Kelsey, my loving appreciation for understanding and supporting, since their childhood, my dedication to the causes of human fairness and social justice. To my co-author, Elizabeth Lynch, thank you for an exciting partnership during the past year and one-half.

Elizabeth: Special thanks to Hildegard Steinbach whose hard work, dedication, loyalty and personal commitment not only played a major part in making this book a reality; but also assisted in sustaining me during some very difficult times. May God continue to Bless and keep her. Finally to Trevor Lee and Dorothy Meekins, you have each in your own way taught me the meaning of "true friendship." Thank you for being my safety net.

# Table of Contents

# Prologue

How many times have you made a suggestion for improving your organization and had it summarily dismissed? Think about watching new employees in your organization who question the way business is conducted and how their enthusiasm wanes after getting the signal not to rock the boat.

How many times have you sat in a meeting and watched an individual's personal agenda override what was best for the organization?

When did you lose your innocence? That is, when did you stop thinking about and creating new ideas for your organization and begin going along just to survive?

If you have ever wondered why you behave the way you do in your organization, you will be interested in this book on how dysfunctional organizational personalities evolve. This is a book about the outrageously poor judgment characterizing the management of many of America's most powerful and supposedly rational organizations. "Experts" have told us that organizational managers are essentially rational beings and that our organizations behave in a rational manner. We know better! Every day when we go to work we see, and participate in, actions undermining the best long-range interests of both ourselves and our organizations. We know something is wrong, but cannot put our finger on it. This is also a book about the American workforce on the edge of the 21st Century and the organizational barriers individuals and groups comprising this "new workforce" encounter. We now know that traditional labor pools are shrinking and members of a "new workforce" — women, persons of color, disabled, and older workers — will replace traditional sources of American labor by the year 2000. Groups comprising this "new workforce" were excluded from the historical development of today's organizational structures and processes, even for that matter from the theoretical foundations governing research on organizational behavior and management practices. They, in short, are encountering exclusionary rather than inclusionary practices based on the assumption that they have to change to "fit" within organizational life. Several distinct elements of an "old paradigm" operate to keep this assumption alive:

> Social Generalizations
> The Illusion of Organizational Rationality
> An Organizational Imperative Valuing Conformity, Malleability, Obedience, and Dispensability

Today most American organizations operate on an old paradigm which stresses similarities, not differences. And, although there are programs like affirmative action, optimistically conceived in the 1960s to bring differing cultural and gender-related perspectives to organizational life, they have not changed the old way of doing things. Perhaps this is because they have been co-opted into support of old paradigm thinking and reinforcement of the status quo.

This book is about discarding the old paradigm, that way of thinking which brought us to where we are today. It is about the idea that the organization is larger and more important than individual considerations; about continuity and historical precedent used to maintain the status quo; about the assumption all groups have to "fit" the old paradigm; about the denial of the reality of the NEED TO CHANGE; and about the barriers to hearing creative new ideas or even admitting they exist.

Finally, this book is about a new paradigm and about how we deal with hitherto unheard voices in the American workforce and the new paths open to us as we look at the changing American workforce. It is about bringing diverse and different opinions together to create a better solution instead of force-fitting them into an existing monolithic view. It is about creating synergy in organizations by allowing them to become more than their parts. It is about encouraging organizational value systems which allow for individual differences and about recognizing that fair and equitable treatment of employees affects organizational vitality and ultimately the bottom line.

We are an instant society — instant meals, instant relationships, instant divorces, instant babies — and this instant society scorns anything we cannot do quickly. Erasing years of history does not happen overnight, but we can and *must* speed up the process of assimilating individuals with different ideas into our organizations in order to become more competitive in a global society. We need a model where people are accepted in our organizations on a faster basis, where socialization means acceptance of individual differences, not conformity to one organizational norm. It is our contention that the more values brought to the organization, the more the organization sees and hears, the more answers the organization generates to solve problems, and the more creative are those answers.

Chapter 1 of this book looks at the Workforce 2000 Challenge and old paradigm assumptions underlying organizational exclusion of the voices of groups comprising Workforce 2000. Chapter 2 examines the "imprinting" of organizational personality, how it develops, and its effect on the organization's ability to adapt to change. Chapter 3 explores the question of whether organizations can change. Chapter 4 contains case studies of the effect of current organizational behavior on diversity and discrimination issues. And, Chapter 5 contains a diagnostic model for solving workforce integration issues enabling organizations to shift to a new paradigm.

\* \* \*

# CHAPTER 1
## The Workforce 2000 Challenge

INTRODUCTION

All across the United States today, a multibillion-dollar tug-of-war pits many major employers against a quickly changing workforce. This unnecessary battle is being fought on the front pages of the nation's newspapers by groups defending or decrying the Civil Rights Act of 1991, or guerrilla-style within organizational ranks. It threatens American productivity, efficiency, and economic leadership and will continue to do so unless we as a nation wise up to what is going on out there.

Americans pride themselves on their ability to cope with seemingly insurmountable challenges. Against all odds, they freed themselves from colonial domination in the eighteenth century, created a model of democracy and ethnic assimilation in the nineteenth, and emerged as the champion of the Free World after 1917. Only in the 1960s did the "land of the free" feel the sting of failure and frustration as symbolized by the Vietnam fiasco. The Grenada and Iraqi campaigns of the 1980s and 1990s seemingly exorcised the demon of Vietnam, but they also helped to disguise a deeper threat to the American way of life.

While Western European managers marched to the tune of "Where Do We Go From Here?" after 1946, American institutional leaders lulled themselves to sleep humming "The Way We Were." Political leaders and scientists mobilized to meet the bogus challenge of world communism. Business and educational leaders relied on advertising and domestic monopolies and went on with business as usual.

In the meantime, things were changing. Since the early 1980s we have heard about the changing workforce, the dramatically different labor market, the 'new workforce' of women, minorities, the economically disadvantaged, the disabled, and older workers, that will replace the shrinking traditional sources of American labor. Today, the courts continue to wrestle with questions of what constitutes employment discrimination toward these groups while reform groups struggle to remove obstacles preventing women, persons of color, the disabled, and older workers from taking advantage of employment opportunities. Their difficulties are magnified because private and public sector organizations have retained the values of an earlier era and are operating in an anachronistic paradigm. As a result, most American organizations are ill-prepared to deal with Workforce 2000 issues.

## 1.  WHAT IS THE OLD PARADIGM?

We have talked about the old paradigm[1] without explaining what it is, where it came from, and defining the underlying assumptions preventing organizations from hearing the voices of groups within Workforce 2000. As we look back to how the modern organization and the old paradigm accompanying its evolution emerged, we need to remember that the workers comprising Workforce 2000, women, persons of color, the disabled, and even older workers (retirement at age 65 was the norm), were not involved in the processes underlying their development.

For most Americans, the organizations crisscrossing the landscape of American life — government, labor unions, educational institutions, charitable enterprises, and legal and health professions — have always existed. We believe these rigid paternalistic, powerful bureaucratic organizations whose workplaces command our lives and demand conformity, malleability, and obedience from their employees have always ruled. Yet, in the early part of the nineteenth century, we see a very different America in which the gigantic bureaucratic public and private sector entities we encounter today were just a glimmer in some futurist's eye.

From approximately the mid-1800s to 1910, U.S. organizations began their slow incremental changes, starting the transformation into today's modern corporations. As the U.S. marketplace moved from the periphery to the vortex of life, American institutions, particularly large-scale businesses like railroads and manufacturing, increasingly integrated their processes. As this transformation took place, labor unions, health facilities, and educational institutions accompanied their growth. Government became the integrator and facilitator for change. And each of these units in its unique way came to emulate the increasingly interrelated processes of large-scale business. In *The Third Wave*, Alvin Toffler has colorfully described the forms and processes organizations adapted to respond to their rapidly changing environment:

> standardization of machines, products and processes; specialization of labor and an even more refined division of labor; synchronization of work into clock time; concentration of energy, population, work education and economic organization; maximization of production; and centralization of power. These principles in turn each reinforcing the other, led relentlessly to the rise of bureaucracy. They produced some of the biggest, most rigid, most powerful bureaucratic organizations the world had ever seen.[2]

As these new administrative bureaucracies appeared, elaborate, formal networks evolved to carefully make and implement long-range plans as well as to direct the organization's day-to-day operations. Formal written rules and clear lines of managerial authority and control were established so people understood their roles, responsibilities, authority, and accountability.

Where traditional organizational control rested in the hands of men deriving power and legitimacy from property ownership and tradition, a different ethic came to prevail in the modern bureaucracy. Control shifted to a management group deriving legitimacy from the increasing professionalization of their positions. This shift brought increasing stress on rationality and efficiency as the new managers, without the power of property or class positions to back them, relied instead on a claim of "efficiency" to justify their power.[3]

The last ingredient in the development of the modern organization and central to our discussion of the old paradigm is its accommodation to the needs and values of able-bodied white male employees under the age of sixty-five. It is not necessary to detail why the needs and values of other groups comprising Workforce 2000 were ignored. One example, however, should prove helpful in demonstrating how the old paradigm operates, the exclusionary principle it maintains, and how we have reached the point today where old paradigm thinking is threatening our very survival. We have had many warning signals from the loss of opportunities to foreign competition to the growing instability of our domestic financial institutions. There were innumerable times when listening to one small voice would have made a difference. Consider the case of the missing refrigerator.

## 2. THE CASE OF THE MISSING REFRIGERATOR

In the early 1960s, a large U.S. home builder expanded operations to include a deluxe custom home division titled Embassy Homes. Instead of cookie-cutter mass-produced housing, the division's goal was to design and build homes appealing to upscale customers. One of its first projects was the development of a large expensive home in the exclusive country club estates section of a southwestern city.

During the home's design and construction, things went smoothly between the all-male architectural and engineering sections of the company, and within a few months the home was completed.

The next step was to ask the home builder's real estate division to begin the sales process. A saleswoman was sent to the home to decide the best marketing strategy. Suddenly what had been viewed as a successful completion of the model for many homes to come became a calamity! During her tour of the home, the saleswoman discovered the kitchen was missing a refrigerator or more to the point, the kitchen was missing a place to put a refrigerator, an oversight on the part of the male architects and engineers. The problem was resolved by placing the refrigerator in the formal dining room, which significantly reduced the selling price of the home.

Today, when we look at the old paradigm resulting from more than a hundred years of evolution of the now anachronistic modern organization, the case of the missing refrigerator symbolizes the missing parts of its development. Just as the sex-segregated workplace excluded important perceptions about the home's design, the exclusion of voices traditionally on the periphery of organizational life — persons of color, women, older workers, the disabled — from the design of modern organizational structures, processes, and theoretical foundations has contributed to the costly upheavals they are experiencing as they grapple with the Workforce 2000 challenge.

## 3. WHAT IS THE CHALLENGE?

*Workforce 2000,* the Hudson Institute Study in 1987, forecasts a significantly different workforce in the decades ahead. It projects a shrinkage of traditional sources of labor while a potential new workforce of women, minorities, disabled, and older workers will fill the void left by reduction in the traditional pool.[4] Although debate has centered on the percentages projected by the Hudson Institute rather than how to meet the challenge of this new workforce, there is consensus that more diversity will characterize America's workforce in the years ahead. Other trends in the country's labor supply portend challenges to American organizations. These include a general shrinking of the workforce, the rise in the average age of workers, more jobs in services and information, and higher skills requirements. To meet all the challenges of this new workforce, innovative strategies and programs are needed to remove obstacles this new workforce now encounters. Few companies in the world will succeed in a few years unless they unleash the excellent talent in diverse populations.

## 4. WHAT ARE SOME OF THE OBSTACLES?

Gender Issues: Because *Workforce 2000* projects almost fifty women in every group of one hundred potential workers, employers will need to consider the special problems women workers face. Among these problems are the "glass ceiling," lack of child and dependent care, pay inequities, and sexual harassment. Creative solutions that are sensitive to these issues will ensure the highest productivity from female employees.

Cultural Barriers: The cultural barriers racial and ethnic groups face today pose many of the same problems women workers encounter, including the "glass ceiling" and pay inequities. Establishing an environment in which a diverse workforce can function to its full potential demands much more than paying lip service to diversity. It requires a change in how the organization listens to groups traditionally outside the mainstream.

Disabled Barriers: Laws like the 1990 Disabilities in Employment Act are increasingly closing the accessibility gap disabled job applicants and workers face. Yet, historic barriers continue to exist for the disabled. Employer perceptions and stereotypes limit recruitment outreach while accommodation issues limit the hiring and promotion of disabled individuals.

Older Workers' Issues: A valuable potential pool of physically and mentally skilled labor, older workers also encounter historical discriminatory barriers in hiring, firing, training, promotion, and benefits. In 1990, age discrimination charges filed with the Equal Employment Opportunity Commission burgeoned to 23,000, up 60% from 1982. One factor that perpetuates discriminatory conduct is the cultural myth that older workers always become less mentally and physically productive with age.

Immigrant and Economically Disadvantaged Barriers: Isolation of many groups in society at large makes their transition to organizational life especially difficult. Here, we are not referring to the structural barriers within organizations, but the very real social obstacles transcending racial and ethnic lines, including deficiencies in basic work and language skills. Physical and social isolation from the work culture, such as found in ghetto neighborhoods or the Ozark Mountains, only exacerbate the existing problem.[5]

## 5. WHY THE OLD PARADIGM FAILS

Using the role of women in the workplace as an example, we can see how and where the concepts of the old model break down and are inappropriate for today's business environment.

Take the case of the missing refrigerator and the absence of women engineers and architects in the design of the home. Predominating stereotypes in the early 1960s based on "biology and destiny" relegated most women to a narrow field of "female" professional occupations: nursing, teaching, library work, clerical, and sales work. If women entered a male-dominated field like engineering or architecture, they rarely received the same treatment accorded their male counterparts. This 1960s sex-segregated workplace has a historical base reaching at least as far back as the advent of the nineteenth century New England factory system. Here we can see the differential employment practices women workers encountered in embryonic form, ranging from job assignments, wages, training, and job mobility to health and safety concerns. Through sheer repetition and the development of the modern organization's regimented personnel systems, these practices became normal procedure by the early part of the twentieth century.

Even in fields they dominated, women were frequently denied top administrative and managerial positions. Existing societal expectations on the distribution of sex roles assumed that women would perform certain indispensable functions such as child-raising and household care, and that their place in the workforce was short-term at best. The impact of war or depression might temporarily change this condition, but these illusionary advances dissipated when the nation returned to normalcy.

Another factor militating against women assuming administrative posts were traits assumed to belong to some men and considered necessary for effective management. Rosabeth Kanter in *Men and Women of the Corporation* identified them: "a tough-minded approach to problems; analytic abilities to abstract and plan; a capacity to set aside personal, emotional considerations in the interest of task accomplishment; and a cognitive superiority in problem-solving and decision - making."[6] These traits were the antithesis of prevailing stereotypes of female behavior as passive, emotional, irrational, and indecisive.

A perusal of business literature offers ample evidence of sexual stereotypes to justify differential and many times subtly discriminatory practices for female workers. Although Title VII of the Civil Rights Act of 1964 seriously challenged discriminatory practices based on sexual stereotypes, many of them still remain. When reviewing the emergence of the modern organizational system, it is apparent that "biology and destiny" played a strong role in excluding women from the development of organizational structures and processes, an exclusion based on stereotypical ideas of women's role in American society and predicated on prevailing social generalizations.

But women are only one example: social generalizations have affected each group represented in Workforce 2000, limiting and distorting perceptions of their character, needs, and contributions. American institutions, laws, and customs provided the environmental context in which these broadly held ideas ensured each group's silence when the modern organization evolved.

Another distinct element of the old paradigm also helps to keep these social generalizations alive — the illusion of organizational rationality. Our culture does not contain concepts for simultaneously thinking about rationality and indeterminateness. This makes it more difficult to assess unreasonable business practices like discrimination masquerading as rational actions. Classical theorists held several identifiable assumptions about the rational behavior of workers which affected the early development of many organizations. Specifically, they viewed workers as reasonable and goal-directed and considered the owner's rights of property more important than, for example, civil rights matters. Rationality was the special province of managers because organizational effectiveness lay with their ability to "fit" individuals into the overall structure. Such design would minimize the irrational efficiency-undermining features of human beings such as unreasonableness, personality, and emotionality.

To their credit, human relationists introduced social and emotional considerations, the human side of organizations, but they did not challenge the image of the rational manager's logical and able control of emotions in the interests of organizational design.[7] Critics, especially Chris Argyris, have questioned these rationalist assumptions on both scientific and moral grounds, but for most of the twentieth century, the assumption of rationality has dominated the development of organizational theory and the evolution of the modern organization.[8]

The Mary Anderson case provides some insights into how the concept of rationality plays in the organization's ability to deal with social generalizations based on race, sex, disability, or age. Anderson was an employee in a large public sector entity. African-American, female, over forty, disabled with asthma and poor eyesight, Anderson drove a van for the Disabled Services Division of the Roads and Highways Department. Throughout her career, she applied for various jobs within the organization with little success, but when the Disabled Services supervisory position opened, she thought this was her opportunity. She had more years of service with the division than any other employee; her training and experience met the requirements for the position; she had substituted for the present supervisor on many occasions and received compliments on her performance; and she had good evaluations on her present job. Imagine Mary's surprise when the Disabled Services Administrator chose a younger, less qualified man for the position.

Outraged, Mary filed a complaint with the Affirmative Action Office. The investigators arranged to discuss the situation with the Disabled Services Administrator and were surprised when they arrived at his office to find on his walls calendars of nude women. They also noted several ethnic and racist jokes tacked on the bulletin board. During the ensuing interview, the investigators learned the administrator's reasons for non-selection included: (1.) Mary did not communicate energetically; (2.) Mary's physical disabilities precluded performance of certain parts of the job; and (3.) Mary did not exhibit the decisive and analytical traits essential for job performance.

After a full investigation which revealed that neither persons of color nor women had ever held supervisory positions in the Disabled Services Division, the investigators sent their determination and recommendations to the head of the Roads and Highways Department. The report stated the Disabled Services selection process for supervisor was invalid based on the standards established by the EEOC Uniform Guidelines on Employee Selection Procedures. The selection process was not validated and operated to discriminate against persons in protected group categories.

When this report reached the head of the Roads and Highways Department, it was discussed and then set aside because to accept the findings would undercut the Disabled Services Administrator's authority. It also would encourage similar complaints from other employees. Mary Anderson took her complaint to the State Attorney General.

Readers probably have many questions about the "real" reasons, the emotional and irrational thoughts, the Disabled Services Administrator had for Mary's nonselection. These questions may include: what the nude calendars and bulletin board material conveyed about the administrator's views of women and persons of color; how he actually felt about the population served by Disabled Services; and what role Mary's age played in his selection. What is very clear from the final disposition of the complaint and not uncommon in organizations, is that top officials minimized the irrationality and emotionality attached to the selection process and how these factors influenced the administrator's views. Rather, they supported his selection as rational and logical and in the best interests of the organization.

The collective mentality of top management and its inability to extricate moral questions in the Mary Anderson case brings us to the third assumption important in our consideration of the old paradigm: the organizational imperative. William Whyte, Jr., brilliantly characterized the special mentality of workers in a large, bureaucratic setting in his *Organizational Man* (1956). He was outraged with the social science role in working hand-in-glove with employers to enforce a manipulative organizational code stressing conformity, getting along with the group, approval from others, and other personality skills. David K. Hart and William G. Scott, in *Organizational America* (1979), placed Whyte's analysis in the broad perspective of organizational values known as the organizational imperative. They maintained that "the modern organization has new values representing a moral commitment in two ways: (1.) all things that are 'good' for Americans come from the modern organization and thus (2.) all individual behavior must conform to the needs of the modern organization."

According to Hart and Scott, the organizational imperative obscures and denies the moral nature of humans in confrontation with systems of order and essentially the tensions inherent in a diverse workforce. Traditional values of the individual ethic (innate human nature, individuality, indispensability, community, spontaneity, volunteerism) are replaced by a collective ethic of malleability, obedience, dispensability, specialization, planning, and paternalism. They acknowledge many Americans still cling to the belief of the individual ethic, but when they enter organizations, they are forced to behave according to the opposite value set. This occurs because modern organizations require obedience to superiors in the hierarchy; they demand that individuals be treated as dispensable resources; they need specialization for efficiency and planning to reduce uncertainty; and they psychologically justify managerial domination by paternalism. The ability of organizations to deny innate human nature, they maintain, has made possible a philosophical view of humanity as completely malleable in a moral sense, and allows people to be viewed as being programmable to any behavioral design required by modern organizations.[9]

Together the organizational imperative, the illusion of organizational rationality, and social generalizations help to keep exclusionary assumptions alive in today's organizations. Springing from the fertile soil of the old paradigm, they enforce similarities and exclude differences. In the process, real change is denied and the status quo becomes the norm.

CONCLUSION

A senior executive of a Fortune 500 company once said, "What happens to us when we get to work? At home we are good people, we have families that adore us, we attend church, we help our neighbors. What happens to us after we back out of the driveway and start that trip to work or school? Maybe we pass through some cloud that changes us. All I know is that I'm always going home on the same route I take to work because I'd hate to take the person I become at work home with me."

Future organizations no longer can use lack of socialization as the reason for not hiring or retaining minorities (the key explanation used in the 80s to describe why most minorities and women could not "make it" in key slots). That excuse worked when the individual's socialization centered around learning and not questioning the status quo. The dynamic environment of today, in which change is the norm, requires that holders of the status quo wake up and realize that the outsiders may hold the key to their successful future. All input is equally valued when a paradigm shifts,[10] but in case after case the holders of the status quo have not recognized their many years of (his)story or (her)story is not buying them much today.

Perhaps if we wait long enough, the problem will resolve itself. The question is, "Can we afford to wait?" What kind of faceless communication can we use in the meantime that will allow all input to be accepted on its merit and not on what the person looks or sounds like. The consequences to organizations attempting change are great and it's only through a new type of thinking that American organizations can maintain a leadership position in the world of tomorrow.

Having examined the exclusion of groups comprising Workforce 2000 from the historical evolution of the modern organization, we now focus on the "imprinting"[11] of organizational personality during this evolutionary process and how it affects the organization's ability to adapt to change.

# CHAPTER 2
## The Obsolete Organizational Personality
### or
## Where Do We Go From Here?

INTRODUCTION

As a fixture in the downtown business section of Tucson, Arizona, for 84 years, Jacome's Department Store enjoyed a reputation for friendliness and honesty. This reputation did not evolve accidentally, but was a well-conceived plan of the store's founder, Carlos Jacome. He believed friendly employees, concern for customer satisfaction, and honesty were the most important elements for attracting customers. Incorporating these ideas into the store's policies and even having them printed on the customer's sales tickets, Carlos refused to carry "seconds" or inferior merchandise, and made it a store policy to accept returned merchandise when it was faulty. As the Twentieth Century advanced and bargain basements became common in most department stores across the country, Jacome's, even after Carlos's demise, refused to sell inferior merchandise, either through a bargain basement or at sales time. There are similar examples across the United States of founders "imprinting" value constructs on their organization which persisted long after they left.[1]

The concept of individual value programming as applied to organizational value development provides insights into the formation of the organizational personality, frequently referred to as organizational "culture." While an organization develops within, and is affected by, the external context of society, internal factors also play a role in the evolution of its culture. One of the major internal factors involved is the founder's value imprint. That imprint contributes significantly to the formation of the organization's systems, structures, and strategies, including human resource policies. Subsequent decision-makers passing through the organization at the same time share similar characteristics and values and translate them into the organizational "right way" to do things in language and action they understand, and of which they approve. Any intrusion from the outside environment on this cozy internal arrangement can threaten both the articulated and unspoken rules and regulations ingrained in the minds of these decision-makers. In fact, the way in which a group responds to external environmental stimuli indicates whether an organization is healthy or dysfunctional in its response to change.

## 1. ORGANIZATIONAL PERSONALITY

What is culture? To most individuals it is an enigmatic concept eluding efforts to get a firm grasp on it. One of our college professors called this "like nailing jello to a tree." Yet culture is very real. It is a system of group beliefs and values determining how a group responds to changes in its internal and external environment. Those responses indicate the group's values or personality.

Culture is wonderful when everyone knows what is expected in order to be part of the "in" group of key decision-makers.

It makes life easier, particularly for those who are success-oriented. It also increases a sense of belonging for those who conform to its dictates, while allowing them to avoid stressful situations. Conversely, culture as a negative force can stop innovation, creativity, and necessary change in the organization.

The root of all organizational personalities lies in the seeds planted by the founder or founders of the group. Their values programmed into the organization shape the direction and attitudes of the organization, persist over time, and can still be found after hundreds of years. An understanding of an organization's history is the key to its personality and the effect of its culture on its behavior in any given circumstance.

## 2. TYPES OF VALUE PROGRAMMING

Humans: Programming of organizational values into group behavior is very similar to the development of human behavior.

According to Dr. Morris Massey, a human behaviorist, 90% of an individual's gut-level values are locked in by the time he or she is ten years old and 100% set at about the age of 20. Massey identifies several stages of personality development, explaining how humans develop and "lock in" their values.[2]

The first stage is imprinting, resulting from the observation of adult behavior by an infant (ages 0 to 7). The infant observes everything around it and uses this information to define the reasons for all the things that exist in the world. This stage is followed by modeling (ages 7 to 10). After observing adult behavior, in its environment, the child will imitate his or her heroes. For example, a very young child repeats things that it hears adults say, and in that way it learns a language. A child also watches adults walk on two feet and wonders "why can't I do that?" Then it will attempt to walk, again modeling the behavior it has seen. After the modeling stage comes socialization when 90% of what the person believes is correct is already stored in his or her brain and shapes the way future choices are made, including the selection of friends. Belonging in this stage is everything, and an individual will seek out others who think, feel, or act the way he/she does. From the child's point of view, this is correct behavior. Longing to be part of a group, a young child will pick the people from whom it wants acceptance and do whatever needs to be done to ensure approval. Either the child finds people who have imprinted and modeled in the same fashion as it has, *or* it changes its behavior to match the group to which it wants to belong.

The last stage of human behavior is socialization or the "locking in" of values, and "lock" is the operative word. Webster's dictionary defines lock "to fasten in or out or to make secure or inaccessible by or as if by means of locks; to hold fast or inactive."[3] Once values are programmed and tested against the reality of the old, the "locked-in" values operate as a filter for viewing the world throughout an individual's life. Anything that fits the filter passes through and is seen or heard, and anything that does not fit is "locked out." Thus, current values are safeguarded.

Groups: Interestingly enough, individuals entering organizations go through the same stages of development as those shaping individual human behavior, only at an accelerated rate. This is due to the fact that unlike a child coming into the world without previous values, adults enter a group after going through all stages of human behavioral development. They have already locked in one set of values, which includes a need for socialization. From the process of learning this set of values, they are able to determine very quickly what they need to do or not to do to become a part of the group. Depending on the individual and the organization, this imprinting period can take place in a matter of days or go on for as long as a year.

For the child modeling is watching and imitating adults around it. The adult entering an organization is not just observing and emulating (modeling) other adults, he/she is also experiencing the results of the group's influence on its members, which translates into a set of values. In other words, the locked-in values of the organization imprinted by its founders influence group norms.[4] For example an entrepreneur starting a company will want that company to reflect his or her personal values. Given the choice, the entrepreneur will probably gather people sharing similar values to the organization since it is essentially an extension of the entrepreneur's personality. Interviews of prospective candidates for organizational membership include measuring them against criteria developed around the values of the entrepreneur. Anyone experiencing rejection after a job interview probably has heard the words, "you're very qualified, but we have found a candidate who better fits our organization." "Fit" is a euphemism for "I'm not sure if you will want to do things the way that we do them." This statement does not mean that your way is wrong. It only means that the person making the decision is looking for an employee who will implement existing procedures, not create new ones. Individuals becoming part of the organization have to choose to exhibit behavior allowing them success in the organization or accept a place at the fringe or outside the group's social systems. The organizational ability to affect an individual's behavior in this fashion is possible because of the human need to be accepted and/or successful. This social need, combined with the organizational imperative of a collectivist mentality, ensures the individual's malleability in adjusting to the organizational personality. An individual becoming this malleable, however, loses the ability to truly "think" beyond what is perceived as acceptable behavior. That trait is stifling to new ideas and is a precursor to problems for an organization in which creativity and innovation are required for success.

## 3. VALUES TURNED INTO PERSONALITY

There are many ways group values can coalesce into personality types. The most common can be characterized as the "Winner's Syndrome," the "Loser's Syndrome," and the "Quick Fix."

### THE "WINNER'S SYNDROME"

Successful organizations spawn employees used to winning and being "on-top." Exhibiting the "Winner's Syndrome," these individuals both imprint and model what they believe is the "right way" to approach markets, develop products, and interact with one another. Once locked in, their values are automatic and routine. There is a camaraderie among those in power and their values permeate the organization. This set of relationships is commonly referred to as the "old boy network."

Overconfident in their ability to win, power brokers imbued with the "Winner's Syndrome" face obsolescence when external environmental changes catch them off guard. Normally at this point a healthy organization seeks advice from outside consultants or hires new people acknowledged as "winners" in the new game. Trouble occurs in the healthy organization when those imbued with the "Winner's Syndrome" are only interested in slight modifications to the old way of doing things. A typical response to these new "right ways" might be, "Jack has some good ideas, but he doesn't understand how we do things here." The basis for this type of response lies in the "classical" approach to management which requires following orders, and not creating new ideas. Innovative ideas are often relegated to the trash bin when the classical manager, incapable of developing an implementation plan without prior experience, labels the new solution as irrelevant, theoretical, or useless.

IBM Chairman, John Akers, stirred up a considerable amount of controversy about worker complacency during the summer of 1991. There were many articles written on the pros and cons of Mr. Akers' complaint that employees of the computer maker were standing around the water cooler waiting to be told what to do while the industry was in crisis.[5] A fair amount of the press put the blame on Mr. Akers. For example:

*His way of trying to shake up the troops hearkens back to the militaristic style of the 1950's. If you can't seem to get things done, you threaten people.*

*To be great as a leader in this situation, Akers should be pointing out what you should be doing. It's good to shake people up once in a while, but then you have to show them what to do differently.*

*Managers have never been told at IBM to challenge what IBM does, to say maybe what we're making is not what the customers want. Now what we have are managers who are used to doing what they are told, not used to coming up with different approaches.*

*I suppose his (Akers') sentiment is fairly widespread among CEO's of many American companies. It is surprising to me that they don't often recognize that the company is the source of the problem.*

*Corporate managers typically learn most of their management techniques on the job.*[6]

How different might these comments have been with the recognition that Mr. Akers was dealing with a workforce suffering from "Winner's Syndrome." Employees in today's environment who are sitting back, waiting for someone to tell them what to do, are exhibiting the values they used to acquire their leadership positions during a growth market. They are still assuming a static, classical environment in which change happens slowly enough for decisions to flow down through hierarchical levels in sufficient time for the implementation of the decision to make a difference. IBM, because of its superior communication systems, can disseminate decisions quickly, but may not be able to change long-held values (behavior) in time to make a difference. Employees and managers today who are specialists waiting for directions to follow are going to be of very little value, now and in the future, for organizations forced into a competitive, fast-paced environment.

The potential for development of an organizational split personality at IBM will increase as new employees entering the organization at crisis mid-point, long-service employees eager for change, and the traditionalists develop differing perceptions of the organization's future. Mr. Akers and IBM are probably at a crossroads. The workforce at IBM will soon consist of some employees who agree with the "new style" and others who still have extreme faith in the organization's ability to survive the latest crisis with old values intact.

## THE "LOSER'S SYNDROME"

Compared to the "Winner's Syndrome," the "Loser's Syndrome" is much more difficult to correct. It occurs with dysfunctional organizational personalities. Here, not only does the organization have to recognize the existence of an environmental problem and deal with it, but it also has to eliminate negative dysfunctional personality characteristics impeding change. These characteristics, such as in-fighting, turf wars, and disinformation to co-workers, create barriers to improvement. It is important that these dysfunctional personality traits be resolved before the organization tackles the environmental threats.

The negative characteristics of a dysfunctional organization are primarily internal and social in nature. Group members will actually feed upon each other due to their fear of being left "out of the loop." This loss of social sanction (not being liked) will cause group members to go to extreme lengths to make sure their status in the organization is not affected. They become irrational and regard unscrupulous, costly, or unreasonable behavior as "normal."

## NEGATIVE DYSFUNCTIONAL
## PERSONALITY CHARACTERISTICS

Healthy organizations tend to be involved in understanding, or are active participants, in their external environment. Dysfunctional organizations, on the other hand, tend to be self-contained. That is, their members are very seldom involved in any outside activities as representatives of the organization. In fact, in some cases individuals active in the external environment will receive criticism from other group members, especially if this involvement gives them visibility in the larger external community.

Dysfunctional organizations rarely invite individuals from outside their organization to provide them any type of information. This is a self-preservation technique allowing the organizational members to live in a self-contained world without the intrusion of outside forces. This may also indicate that the group is aware of its dysfunctional attributes and is reluctant to hold its values up to the scrutiny of outsiders. This organizational fear of being compared to the outside world is the same type of fear that people exhibit if an unwelcome visitor attempts to enter their locked home. The intrusion poses a problem, and like different individual responses of flight or fight, some organizations flee by ignoring the signs of the external intrusion, while the truly dysfunctional organizations will go to extreme measures to resist the efforts from the outside force. Two examples follow:

> *An individual seen in one group as a "fast tracker" enters another organization at a very senior level and is clearly in line for one of the top three positions in the company when the incumbents retire. Competitors for the same slot freeze this individual out of the mainstream, facilitate errors in his department by providing misinformation, make decisions that affect him without his knowledge, and in general create problems for him to solve. In less than 14 months, this previously highly respected individual is seen as not capable of handling the responsibility assigned and is dismissed for cause.*
>
> *During a recent seminar, an employee in a dysfunctional organization posed a hypothetical question. The employee did not believe that the workers could fix problems as long as they were forced to do what they (management) wanted them to do. When advised that he surely had a choice to do what was right and was only limited by his willingness to take risks, he replied, "Sure, it's easy for you to say that, or for those individuals who can afford to move, or have someone to protect them. Barring that protection, you have to go underground and make changes any way you can." When asked "what happens when you have a whole company operating that way?," he laughed and asked, "Are we still talking hypothetically?" It is important to note that his company RARELY if EVER fires employees, but those out of favor are left out of important decisions, or not invited to key meetings.*

The modern classical organization requires obedience to superiors in the chain of command, and all individuals outside the decision-making loop are treated as dispensable resources. It encourages specialization and efficiency and it psychologically justifies paternalistic managerial domination as the appropriate solution for organization survival. Far too many classical thinkers have lost sight of the fact that the basic reason for going to work is to make a product or to provide a service, not to use the organization as the vehicle for achieving social status. Human resource systems failing to address the "social" needs of employees will never touch the critical question of an individual's need for social status and its effect upon the employee's ability to be a valuable contributor to the product/services needs of the organization. Nor will it address the special needs of Workforce 2000 as individuals with different views try to assimilate into these closed organizations.

### THE "QUICK FIX"

When faced with the need to make organizational change, managers who have spent all their lives in a "classical" environment invariably try the "Quick Fix" approach. They read everything they can on what is "hot" in organizational theory and then adopt it, hoping they have picked the right solution.

"So what?" you are probably saying to yourself. "This phenomenon is a natural part of life. With this approach, everyone suffers equally and no one seems to have found a better way." This reaction is perfectly natural (everyone experiences it at one time or another), but it is the beginning of resistance to change. When exhibited in organizations, such mental blocks become the barriers to change. Their relationship to the next decade's diverse workforce issues is especially significant because many people talk about diversity without understanding what that means in terms of changes in the basic foundation of organizational systems.

Managers trained in the classical environment have learned how to act according to organizational precepts, not to create; thus this emphasis on the passion for "quick fixes." These managers do not have the critical problem-solving skills necessary to assess different situations on their own merit.

In the absence of these skills, classical managers must resort to adopting solutions that they know have worked in the past. When a new problem requiring a creative solution is presented, classical practitioners blindly try to hide their lack of knowledge. They take steps to silence suggestions that do not match their paradigms, mainly because they lack the skills to assess their validity. "Quick Fix" individuals rarely consider the long-term implications of solutions. They live in the "here and now" and worry only about today or their personal growth horizon. These managers are not lacking in intellect. On the contrary, "Quick Fix" addicts are usually highly intelligent and skilled, but they are operating with limited fields of vision and tend to be more concerned about social status and personal gain than organizational goals and objectives.

## 4. DYSFUNCTIONAL ORGANIZATIONS

Many people believe that organizations cannot change because they accept the idea that changing culture is too complex a process to undertake. Their assumption is that there are too many people involved. The fallacy in this is the belief that many individual personalities must be dealt with, when in reality members of a group normally operate with a common mind and personality. If a dysfunctional organization is analyzed and addressed as a single mind, solutions become clearer. Groups of people who have imprinted, modeled, and socialized in the same timeframe and the same environment will have primarily the same set of values. An individual who imprints or models in a dysfunctional environment can take on its dysfunctional values. The collective behavior, given an understanding of how the collective values were programmed, is just as predictable as individual human behavior.

A considerable amount of published research exists on personality and human behavior and how to correct so-called inappropriate behavior. The determination of what behavior patterns to change is one of the necessary first steps in helping an individual recognize that a problem exists. A trained therapist will sometimes spend years delving into a person's past to discover where or how the behavior began and what past events may have caused the present dysfunctional problems.

Dysfunctional groups must go through a process similar to this individual examination, but at a faster pace. Groups, like individuals need to look at the past, in this case the organizational history, and find what actions are actually causing present problems. This is necessary because individuals comprising these groups have absorbed the organization's dysfunctional values in order to survive. In the absence of other models they consider their dysfunctional and irrational behavior as normal. Why their own personal values do not help them avoid this trap is a logical question, but in most cases it is because they are consumed with their own survival. This may explain why large numbers of white collar workers today are experiencing stress symptoms. Literally everyone in a dysfunctional organization knows what is going on and will either participate in order to gain acceptance, or will stand by and watch, afraid to voice real opinions. Workers on the periphery of this system are more likely to speak up and challenge the "status quo." Why? Because, unlike those in the organizational mainstream, they have never been included in the social systems and therefore have little to lose by challenging them.

Too often, individuals and groups wrestling with diversity issues ignore the root causes for dysfunctional behaviors and simply try to take the new and shape it to "fit" the old paradigm. This patchwork approach ignores the need to change and to adopt a new paradigm. Increasingly these old paradigm adherents will find their perceptions and values challenged by demographic shifts in the workplace. For example, today some experts maintain that successful managers are operating with a new style which has more stereotypically feminine than male attributes . . . a clear reflection of a paradigm shift. Another example is the debate over the Civil Rights Act of 1991. Old paradigm thinkers argued that this legislation would provoke massive discrimination charges and create an undue burden on society. It probably did not occur to them that as the workforce becomes more diverse and Workforce 2000 employees encounter holders of the status quo and their old paradigm obsolete values, more discriminatory actions could take place.

## 5. AFFIRMATIVE ACTION IN DYSFUNCTIONAL ORGANIZATIONS

Affirmative action is not a new concept. It first appeared in 1961 when President John F. Kennedy issued Executive Order 10925. That order established the President's Commission on Equal Employment Opportunity and required Government contractors to take affirmative action to find and employ qualified women and members of minority groups. In 1965, President Lyndon B. Johnson issued Executive Order 11246, as amended, requiring companies with federal contracts to develop affirmative action programs. Department of Labor guidelines in 1970 emphasized that such programs should be result-oriented. Revised Order 4 in that same year required a workforce analysis and the setting of goals and timetables to ensure "good faith efforts." Rather than absolute numbers, these goals and timetables were to be an estimate of what the workforce might reflect if equal opportunity and nondiscrimination had been historically applied. Later federal legislation added handicapped and disabled/Viet Nam veterans to affirmative action programs. Whereas a utilization cap applied to the recruitment and selection of qualified women and minorities proportional to their presence in the marketplace, affirmative action for the physically challenged and disabled/Viet Nam veterans was to be continuously applied without regard to goal-setting.

Perhaps no area of equal employment law is more misunderstood than affirmative action. It is a program to rectify past discrimination, intentional and unintentional, for women, racial and ethnic minorities, the physically challenged and disabled/Viet Nam veterans. Employers take steps to include these groups in their workforce through result-oriented planned outreach good faith efforts. Simultaneously, organizations seek to assure an internal climate which facilitates employment and retention of protected group members. An affirmative action program also ensures equal opportunity and nondiscrimination. Equal opportunity simply means an employer must provide opportunities for all qualified persons, and individuals are judged on their ability to meet the requirements of the job. Nondiscrimination is a condition that does not give preference to or deny persons employment because of their race, color, religion, national origin, age, veteran's status, handicap, or sex.

Equal opportunity and nondiscrimination are integral to an affirmative action program. Together these concepts reinforce the organizational need to demonstrate a respect for all people and their capabilities. Often because the affirmative action concept is inappropriately applied, equal opportunity and non-discrimination are negated. This may happen in closed organizations closely tied to the old paradigm where the residuals of the industrial competitive win/lose adversarial ideas dominate work life. Failure to establish fair and equitable standards for human resource functions makes these organizations even more susceptible to abusing equal opportunity, nondiscrimination and affirmative action. The absence of such standards enables these organizations to manipulate their human resource systems and, in the process, violate the rights of all groups. Unfortunately, inadequate or corrupt affirmative action programs can facilitate the exclusion of women and minorities in dysfunctional organizations. Some of the characteristics of such affirmative action programs which immediately signal dysfunctional problems are:

1) Organizational denial the program is needed, although gross violations of equal employment opportunity and affirmative action regulations are clearly apparent;
2) Limitation of resources and assignment of inexperienced people to implement the program;

3) Exclusion of the program from decision-making processes;
4) Assignment of protected group members to positions with long titles which carry little responsibility or where responsibilities are not equal to those of their peers;
5) Creation of new positions for protected group members who usually have to write their own job descriptions;
6) A tremendous emphasis on numbers, which allows the organization to stay on the fringe of meeting affirmative action and equal employment opportunity regulations and to pay very little attention to the people behind the numbers;
7) Placement of protected group members in staff functions, but rarely in key decision-making slots;
8) Continuing problems with pay equity issues;
9) Violation of the basic concepts of laws governing protected groups by human resource policies;
10) Minimal or no utilization of minority firms to supply products and/or services.

Individuals and groups are pitted against each other in this atmosphere, and the equal opportunity directive of "qualified" becomes an operative word. For example, qualified can be erroneously defined as fitting the values of the old paradigm. It can also connote a historic undervaluation of protected groups and thereby play an important role in preserving distorted views of their potential as employees.

## 6. ORGANIZATIONAL CHANGE

Just as in human beings, the organization's personality is a system of beliefs and values which determine its ability to create change. The more successful these beliefs and values have been in the past, the more difficult the change. What happens when past success dictates future actions? Joel Barker, a futurist, discusses this concept in his book on paradigms titled, *Discovering The Future*. Paradigms are "patterns which are the sum total of an individual's experiences, or their view of the world." Barker uses this concept along with Thomas Kuhn's *Structure of Scientific Revolutions* to show how individuals develop mental blocks which literally stop them from being able to process information that does not fit their current paradigm. According to Barker, when a major environmental change takes place, paradigms shift and all those impacted by that paradigm lose any advantage created by their previous knowledge. He calls this the "going back to zero" point.[7] The 1991 Civil Rights debate makes salient the numbers who do not recognize a paradigm shift is taking place. While this bill is designed to affect all of us — Whites, Blacks, Hispanics, Asians, Indians, religious groups, older workers, the disabled — "classical" thinkers by focusing on what they may have to give up, do not realize they are at the starting line with everyone else. Environmental factors are major determinants of the impact on gut-level value structures at both the individual and the group level.

Private and public sector organizations in a stable environment, looking for incremental changes over a long period of time, can afford to follow past patterns and practices. If, due to a major environmental shift, they find themselves in serious trouble, tried and true methods may not prove efficacious. Further complications result if the change needs to occur in a short period of time or if the organization has a dysfunctional personality.

## 7. CONCLUSION

The classical approach is appropriate and workable in organizations when the environment is stable and the rate of change is measured in years. In a dynamic environment where change is measured in increasingly shorter increments, the classical concept resembles a fortress manned or womaned by guards who determine who does or does not gain entry into the organizational mainstream — a process which, at best, slows the rate of change and, at worst, gridlocks the whole organization.

Our survival and that of our institutions is dependent on what we see and hear. If managers resist change patterns and continue blindly within the confines of the past, the final cost is organizational demise. Organizations must determine how to remove obstacles limiting newcomers, whether because of protected group status or previous organizational experiences, and include them as contributors to the mainstream. Accomplishing this is the key to turning Workforce 2000 into a winning strategy. For centuries we have labored with the assumption that in order for me to win, you had to lose. Win/lose as a concept dominated human relationships. Barring an unforeseen natural disaster or a man-made catastrophe, the future will arrive. The Western World will pass through the transformation point in the next few years. It will be an age of multiple choices, offering no more basic true or false questions. "Quite possibly it could be 'E' — all of the above, an age in which opposites can work and co-exist."[8]

An understanding of organizational personality, its history and impact, leads to yet another question: whether dysfunctional organizations can change their personalities. We can answer this question in part by stating that the more negative values exhibited by the organization, the more difficult it is for change to take place. In the next chapter we examine dysfunctional values and the many inherent problems they present in organizations from the perspective of an affirmative action program.

# CHAPTER 3
## Can Personalities Be Changed?

INTRODUCTION

Once upon a time, two large organizations existed side by side in the same city. The founders of Organization "A" surrounded themselves with highly capable individuals of all races and both sexes. The physically-challenged and older employees found the organizational environment very supportive. Through fair and equitable employment policies and practices, equal employment and nondiscrimination prevailed. There was an open environment within the organization which contributed to respect and trust among the members; and the group worked well together, with each person lending his or her expertise and support to the others.

The founders of Organization "B," although paying lip service to nondiscrimination and equal opportunity, maintained a closed environment and hired individuals like themselves. They placed little value on the capabilities of persons covered by equal employment laws, believing they were incapable of performing the intricate and highly intellectual work of the organization. The underlying sentiment was that such persons could only weaken organizational effectiveness. There were visible persons of color and females strategically placed for cosmetic effect, but they were excluded from the decision-making processes.

One day, each organization received a mandate requiring it to develop a written affirmative action plan. Although both organizations were on tight budgets, Organization "A" immediately introduced an innovative program to resolve any problems discovered during the plan's development. Organization "B" denied there was a need to "really" implement its affirmative action plan and put an inexperienced staff member from Human Resources in charge. He immediately encountered insurmountable obstacles.

Within a year, Organization "A" completely resolved its problems and moved on to implementing programs to enhance its management of diversity. Organization "B" had hired a few individuals from underrepresented groups to meet its affirmative action goals. One of these was a talented black employee, John Young. John had graduated from college with honors and was anxious to prove himself. When he reported to work the first day, he noticed that some of the employees were cool to him, but he chalked that up to his newness and felt things would change after he got started on his projects. He planned to keep a low profile and try to fit in. Two years later, he was still trying.

In both Organizations "A" and "B," fairness and equity values were set or locked in long before any legal mandate to establish an affirmative action program appeared. John Young's experience could have been substantially different if he had entered Organization "A." A fairness standard was integral to that organization's culture, giving total valuation to individuals whatever their background, gender, culture, race, religion, or disability. Such a standard can be part of an organization's culture, as in the case of "A," or fostered by change agent programs like affirmative action.

The question is whether Organization "B" can change. This is open to interpretation and depends on how it processes and utilizes information. If, for example, its paradigm, its world view, is open to new information and has flexibility to utilize this information to create change, then Organization "B" will deal with its behavior. Conversely, if Organization "B" is a closed system which screens out new information that cannot be processed within its existing paradigm, it will have great difficulty coping with change. According to Anne W. Schaef and Diane Fassel, *The Addictive Organization*, such organizations may publicly espouse the belief change is possible and desirable, while in reality they are singularly dedicated to stasis.[1] Negative values are so deeply ingrained in these systems that they are invisible to the naked eye. Such systems refuse to allow in, or even recognize, information that cannot be processed within their existing paradigm and many times the seriously systematically disordered organization requires major surgery before change can occur.

There may be persons in Organization "B" with a commitment to pluralism. Indeed, some of the organizational leaders may expound at great length and with extreme integrity about their efforts. But, as Publisher David Lawrence of *The Miami Herald* commented at a February 1990 Knight-Ridder Management Conference, "I'm no cynic, but I tell you — with weariness — that today it is the well-meaning people who are often the problem. The well-meaning people are often the real barriers to real progress — I have come to the conclusion, beaten into me by experience, that before we can *really* make progress, you and I need to confront ourselves. Rhetoric is inexpensive — results are what count."[2]

In order to create change, organizations must first recognize their dysfunctional symptoms and the reasons for their failure to create an organizational environment that works for everyone. They have to penetrate the irrational behaviors at work — the denial, dishonesty and confusion — which block recognition of the problem. When dealing with Workforce 2000 issues these unhealthy behaviors become especially salient seen through the lens of a change agent program like affirmative action.

Volumes have been written on affirmative action programs as a strategy for helping organizations meet their social, moral, and legal obligations to provide a fair and nondiscriminatory workplace. Today, however, these programs are negatively perceived in many quarters. Whatever engendered these adverse reactions is open to debate, but one point is clear. If the organization is still operating in old paradigm patterns which reinforce irrational discriminatory behavior, if the organization has failed to adopt a fairness standard which includes equal opportunity and nondiscrimination, and if the organization sanctions the dysfunctional aspects of its regular system which militate against the inclusion of diverse groups, then it will have problems sustaining an effective affirmative action program. It will also have great difficulty reaching the next plateau of valuing and managing an empowered diverse workforce.

The Stonewall University affirmative action study which follows demonstrates how negative values and avoidance of fairness issues are woven into the organizational fabric, how these values are manifested through organizational leaders and members, and the overall unhealthy symptoms displayed by a dysfunctional organization.

## 1. THE CLOSED SYSTEM AND IRRATIONALITY

Many organizations have difficulty recognizing processes which reinforce discriminatory behavior. This is especially true for dysfunctional organizations, where everyone experiences the negative impact of unfair practices. Programs encouraging diversity represent change for protected groups which ultimately enhance an organization's employment practices for all groups. Yet, when faced with pressures to change, a systemically disordered organization will maintain the status quo through infinite varieties of bureaucratic deception and self-deception which distort every aspect of organizational life.[3]

The Stonewall University case study combines actions of several organizations threatened with change to show how organizational dysfunctional behavior actually manifests itself. This case study is especially revealing for the issue of affirmative action and for dealing with Workforce 2000 issues because it illustrates how organizational change programs dealing with diversity are subverted to support the status quo. It is an almost universal belief that colleges and universities take leadership on questions concerning social change. This belief is, of course, balanced by a counterview that higher educational institutions reflect American society in microcosm. In reality, these institutions comprise a state within a state, where internal customs and mores govern day-to-day activities. As public entities, however, they have an obligation to conduct themselves in an honest and forthright fashion, and if they have enunciated support for pluralism, they have an obligation to follow through on that commitment. In a healthy society, people say what they want and need and then they listen to others' needs and negotiate solutions acceptable to all. Systemically disordered organizations revert to manipulation, power plays for control, distorted communication, dishonesty, and other tactics to maintain the status quo.[4] This is what happened in the Stonewall University case.

Although higher educational institutions are society's repositories for critical intellectual inquiry, many, like other American organizations, have had difficulty understanding and applying the principles of affirmative action. During the years affirmative action programs were becoming the norm for many higher educational institutions across the United States, Stonewall University paid scant attention to the issue. Established in the late 19th Century by legislators and local businessmen and still an institution where the values of this earlier era prevailed, Stonewall resisted incorporation of equal opportunity and affirmative action guidelines into its policies and procedures. In the late 1960s and early 1970s, it began attracting distinguished scholars and large numbers of federal grants, but continued to ignore civil rights mandates. Consequently, its affirmative action program consisted of little more than submission of regular statistical reports to the Office of Federal Contract Compliance Programs (OFCCP) and the Equal Employment Opportunity Commission (EEOC). In 1983 the state's Civil Rights Commission held a public hearing on the university's lack of equal employment opportunity and affirmative action efforts. This brought increased community pressure on the institution to improve its program. At the same time the OFCCP warned the university it would lose its federal contracts unless it cleaned up its act.

Reacting to this pressure, Stonewall's president, Heine "Dutch" Heineken, established an affirmative action office with its director, Don Smith, reporting directly to him. Smith had wide-ranging experience in the development and implementation of affirmative action programs, and his appointment was enthusiastically greeted by the community. Internal reaction to Smith's appointment and the establishment of the affirmative action office was swift and negative. Faculty members extolled the virtues of the university's commitment to affirmative action and argued that the program was not needed because the institution had practiced it since the day it was founded. Administrators stated they were already sensitive to the issues and to deal daily with the new program would interfere with their operations. Staff members, perhaps the most honest of the three groups, declared their fear that the program jeopardized their upward mobility within the university system. "Outsiders" had caused the university to take a look at its employment practices and were demanding change take place. For university "Insiders," "Outsiders" were not welcome.

In contrast, healthy organizations are open to criticism and if change is necessary, look for corrective actions. A healthy reaction in the Stonewall case requires administrators, faculty, and staff to acknowledge the need to make their organization work for everyone. Since a large volume of complaints exists about the institution's lack of either equal opportunity or affirmative action, they would begin to look for arbitrary barriers to diversification of their workforce and seek fair and equitable recruitment and hiring procedures, upward mobility systems, and training programs.

In a moral sense, healthy organizations recognize the example they set for others. In a legal sense, public organizations recognize the expense they cause taxpayers when they fail to eliminate discriminatory practices, while private sector employers are well aware of how such lawsuits affect their bottom line. It is the practical economic imperative, if nothing else, that should motivate organizations to rethink their behavior on diversity issues. This is true whether the organization is a newspaper appealing to diverse readership or an educational institution recruiting a multicultural student body. The need for diverse perspectives, the inclusion of voices unheard in the past is essential to reach the markets of tomorrow.

Stonewall's institutional philosophy statement included the encouragement of an awareness and appreciation of diverse backgrounds. It was verbally reinforced by the mission statement specifying cultural diversity as an institutional goal. Neither university policies nor procedures incorporated this goal. Lack of cultural diversity characterized both the staff and student body. On paper, the university declared that multicultural and diversity issues guided its efforts, and many of its employees believed this organizational myth and were hooked on its promise. However, its unstated goal was, "please don't bring change to this campus because we don't want to deal in practice with our stated goal of pluralism." Many employees and students failed to see how the system really worked. Consequently, believing in the promise of the university's mission, they felt that it did not need an affirmative action program.[5] Opponents of the program's implementation adroitly used these perceptions to buttress their arguments against it — not unusual behavior in a dysfunctional organization.

Healthy organizations do not act this way. They understand the need for congruence between their mission and their operative stated and unstated goals. Unambiguous goals exert a strong healthy influence and serve as a rallying point and an inspiration for organizational members while reducing political cleavages and conflict. Ultimately organizational effectiveness is inextricably tied to goal congruence and the coping with environmental uncertainty.

The lack of congruence between the university's stated goal and its actual practice gridlocked the organization into a rigid denial system.[6] The new affirmative action officer faced a wall of resistance which, like a hydra, reached into every corner of the institution. Moving immediately to a systematic review of the history of the university's affirmative action program, he discovered that most of the records had disappeared. No one seemed to have information on the subject except the Institutional Operations Director. This man had been with the university for three decades and was well-known for his secretive ways. He revealed to the affirmative action officer that in previous years, Stonewall had made a few attempts at recruitment and selection of diverse groups, but the campaign very quickly lost momentum. Apparently the absence of historical documentation is a classical dysfunctional symptom reflecting institutional disinterest in the issue because if something did not exist, it simply did not have to be considered. According to Schaef and Fassel, "in closed systems, information that cannot be processed within the existing paradigm will not be allowed in or recognized." Loss of memory is part of this process and the unwillingness to learn from past mistakes assures the replication of old patterns and nonsolutions.[7]

Smith found this denial system had militated against development of university policies and procedures to deal with discrimination. Several reports on the status of women on university campuses detailed some of the problems. Inequity in recruitment, tenure, retention, and promotion headed the list of problems for female faculty and staff. The reports singled out career development problems, including the lack of performance evaluations, career paths, and equitable awarding of honors to women on campuses. They also contained detailed descriptions of a "chilly" climate on many campuses for culturally diverse women and the physically challenged.

Smith knew the university needed a plan for its investment in human capital. It lacked fair and equitable standards in its human resources policies, with the clearest example being a weak compensation and classification system. Almost one-half of the staff and administrative positions lacked job specifications. Smith proposed a study to determine solutions for the problem.

He also began a review of employee handbooks and found material violating federal laws and regulations. Particularly concerned with the inadequate grievance procedures in the manuals and their blatant disregard for timeliness and due process, Smith instituted temporary procedures to accommodate the large number of complaints, including sexual harassment, flooding into his office. When he reported these complaints to administrative personnel, he found they used a variety of repressive strategies to avoid confronting the problem: Nonaction, "administrative orbiting" which meant holding matters "under advisement," and secrecy.[8] Smith also became aware of administrators' blindness to a broad array of other personnel problems in the areas they controlled. This was probably because they rarely left their offices to mingle with students and staff.

Healthy organizations consider a plan for investment in diverse human resources essential for an organizational environment that works for everyone. Executives and administrators are intimately aware of, and involved in, this plan. They are also concerned that equitable human resource policies reflect a basic organizational standard of fairness. Poor grievance procedures, or lack of procedures, to address inequities only exacerbate existing tensions. As the CEO of a healthy organization explained, "Doing what is right requires letting conflict surface. Sure the natural thing for management to do is to be upset and angry and not do a thing and try to shove it down. Ultimately, what happens is that people aren't listened to and they are clearly driven away."[9]

Because the existing affirmative action plan of Stonewall University lacked goals and timetables, Smith developed a new plan and presented it to university administrators at an official meeting. They attacked the plan as statistically unreliable. They also refused to accept the plan's strong responsibility statement which placed the burden of results squarely on their shoulders. The president, although publicly stating his support for the plan, agreed with his administrators behind the scenes. Compare these reactions to the statement of a CEO seeking to diversify his staff: "I focus on attitudes, not numbers. If you are a manager, you specifically must show progress each year in pluralism. That is partly how managers are evaluated for salary increases."[10]

It was obvious that there had been no previous training about equal employment standards governing job interviews for university employees. Ignorant of the violations they committed, campus selection committee members often manipulated requirements and interviews for a particular favorite "inside" candidate. Smith trained equal opportunity coordinators for university departments to serve on search committees and support departmental efforts in making affirmative action outreach. Very few were utilized. Immediately following the hearing held by the Civil Rights Commission, the university president assembled a coalition of community and campus leaders to launch an educational program entitled, "Diversity Now." Smith saw this program as a vehicle to begin a needed discussion of diversity issues on the campus. Much to his dismay, within months the budget for the new program was slashed from $80,000 to $15,000. By that time the program was no longer newsworthy. This program was one of several which the university utilized to create a media image of its support for diversity issues. This image, of course, diverted attention from internal problems.

Compounding difficulties in resolving technical problems were the negative behaviors and attitudes underlying them. The conduits for both were the campus informal and formal communication systems. Communication processes at the university were marred by a stubborn inability to confront the truth. A vague, confused and ineffective communication system formed a vehicle for distortion of facts. Gossip and "secrets" constituted a steady diet for campus personnel, and they spent a great deal of time trying to find out what was "really" going on at Stonewall. The fact is very little was happening at the university. Administrators made it a habit to deal with each other in memo form because memos helped them avoid face-to-face confrontation on touchy issues. They also used memos to document events when under attack before the manipulation of cloudy organizational memory changed the facts. Personalizing of issues was a regular occurrence, and administrators were particularly sensitive to scapegoating. Two levels of communication existed throughout the campus: what was said and what was meant.[11]

Misinformation and secrets are the special province of unhealthy organizations. Everything an organization does revolves around a process of communication, and opportunities abound for blocking or distorting communication if the organization is determined in that direction. Such behaviors can include manipulating perceptions, erroneous translations, distortions from the past, defensive tactics, and a general lack of congruence. Ultimately, "as a system becomes sicker, it becomes more rigid and dishonest. It uses denial to avoid seeing its reality. In fact, it creates its own reality."[12]

In comparison, healthy organizations rely on employees' ideas, conflicts, and reactions as a rich source of continual change.

Publisher David Lawrence states, "If you've got bad news, give me the bad news and I'll work from there. There's almost always more than one way to do something. It's often a matter of communication. It's terribly healthy for employees to be able to ask questions. I've got nothing to hide. I'd rather deal with the information or misinformation straightforwardly."[13]

Every day complainants streamed into Stonewall's affirmative action office. In the previous year alone, the university had spent close to one million dollars defending discrimination suits in state and federal courts, and Smith knew internal mediation could considerably reduce this sum. He also cited the need for developing a healthy internal climate focusing on human resource planning, the use of managerial solutions rather than defensive legalistic maneuvers, and the effective utilization of employees as proactive means for the long-term reduction of grievances. No one heard him. University attorneys continued to adhere to a "let 'em sue" philosophy. Arrogant administrators only compounded the problem.

One of Smith's first complainants was Ralph Wing, an Assistant Professor in the Biological Sciences Department. Recently denied promotion and tenure, Wing charged the University with racial discrimination. The day after he filed with the affirmative action office, Wing's complaint made headline news in the local newspaper. Discussion on campus revolved around the personalities of those involved in the Wing case. Strong support existed for both administrators responsible for the decision, the Dean of Liberal Arts, and the Vice President for Academic Affairs. They refused to reconsider their denial of Wing's tenure. A few persons outside the "Insider's" circle took Wing's side. In the meantime, Smith found himself in the middle, actually becoming the scapegoat for the whole affair. Wing continued to make public pronouncements about the matter, to the embarrassment of the president. A crisis had erupted.

Crises were regular occurrences at Stonewall. A classic behavior for confused dysfunctional systems, crises temporarily focus attention away from the constancy of this confusion. Like people in a nation at war, employees inside dysfunctional systems set aside their conflicts and differences to work toward conquering the enemy. In the Stonewall case, an illusionary feeling of solidarity pervaded the campus while the president and a few faculty and administrators took several abnormal actions to control the situation. During crises, such irregular managerial actions are excused as essential while in reality they heighten the organization's tolerance for daily dysfunctional behavior. Ultimately crises reduced Stonewall's ability to plan or take responsibility for its actions. Crises fed the illusion that cracking down can bring the situation under *control* while enabling management to "assume an unhealthy amount of power on a daily basis."[14]

Interestingly, R. Roosevelt Thomas, Jr., *Beyond Race and Gender*, has attributed crisis management to the limitation of affirmative action efforts. He states, "there is a frustrating and virtually unavoidable cycle (with affirmative action programs) which inevitably creates a cycle of crisis, problem recognition, action, great expectations, disappointment, dormancy, and renewed crisis."[15] Apparently the Stonewall affirmative action case is just one more example of how many organizations have dealt with the issue.

In the Stonewall crisis, personalities as usual took center stage in the controversy. Again, personality conflicts successfully diverted attention from the real issue, discrimination. When Wing received an offer from another university, the conflict subsided, but the whole question of affirmative action had taken on new meaning. Other problems were multiplying for Smith as well. He wondered if he could establish any part of the affirmative action program. Blocked at every turn, he felt powerless to implement change.

## THE EFFECT OF EXECUTIVE LEADERSHIP ON ORGANIZATION CHANGE

Like the founder's imprint, the value constructs of persons holding powerful positions vitally affect the organization's culture. The more powerful the positions persons occupy in the organization, the more their individual value commitments can mold the organizational culture and determine its ethics. In fact, the real role of chief administrators is to manage the values of the organization because its cultural values are central to excellent performance. Organizational change mechanisms must emanate from those directly charged with shaping policy, and this same executive power is utilized through influence and communication networks to carry out policy changes. As one top executive explained, "Change can't bubble up from the bottom. Maybe some good stuff can emerge, but the folks you've got to get to are the ones running the institutions."[16]

If executives actively buy into irrational behavior and the status quo, their behavior may not only prove counterproductive, but perhaps fatal, bringing the organization to the brink of destruction. In the closed system, short-term political gains can eclipse the longer executive view. Narrow interests can crowd out broader concerns and obscure any ethical visions inclusive of, or committed to, a broader community. As the closed system feeds on itself, the dysfunctional aspects of executive leadership are multiplied.[17]

Dr. Heine "Dutch" Heineken, the president of Stonewall University, had held several administrative positions within the institution and was noted for his ability to survive the frequent crises which engulfed it. He had rarely shown interest in affirmative action and equal employment and, in private conversations, voiced his opinion that the program was a "necessary evil." To comply with the new demands and with great public fanfare, he did place a few women, minorities, and physically challenged persons in highly visible positions with little authority. "Dutch" also initiated a special program to address affirmative action goals, but arbitrarily utilized the program to take care of his personal and political debts. Among the appointments under this program were a sprinkling of protected group members, but because of the political nature of their hiring and the violation of both nondiscrimination and equal employment principles, Heineken's actions only fueled "quota" rhetoric across the campus.

"Dutch" used an effective ploy to keep opponents off balance. Because gossip and rumor ran rife through the organization, he utilized this organizational habit to develop negative perceptions of his enemies. The tactic worked well and created a great deal of confusion about the capabilities of targeted individuals while ultimately invalidating their effectiveness. In contrast, organizational leaders in healthy institutions encourage conflicting views to surface and regard this as the way to reach solutions that work. They also see organizational strength tied to the honesty with which the organization deals with a diversity of opinions.

Barraged by demands from faculty, staff, and administrators to "do something" about the affirmative action program before it caused more problems and at the same time embarrassed by the Wing affair, "Dutch" began holding meetings and brainstorming sessions with his top administrators. Executives in dysfunctional organizations are exceptionally adept at using such meetings to cover up real problems. Thus, what ensued was an endless series of meetings from which a skillful avoidance of confronting the issue finally led "Dutch" to the Institutional Operations Director. He asked the Director to develop a plan to "appear" to comply with community demands without upsetting internal groups. This Director was well known not only for his secrecy, but also for his selective sampling of information. He sampled narrowly inside and outside the institution, and he chose very carefully his sources of information and advice. As a result, while his plans usually gave the impression of encouraging change, in reality they perpetuated the status quo.[18]

The Institutional Operations Director surveyed and selectively interviewed students, faculty, staff, and administrative officers and with his help "Dutch" reached a final decision. He would solve his problems by "restructuring" the affirmative action office and remove Smith from it. Moving the office under the Vice President for Academic Affairs, "Dutch" transferred Smith to a dead-end position in the Institutional Operations Director's office. When asked about Smith's reassignment, the president replied that "his unique talents and expertise were required elsewhere at this time."

Smith was replaced by the new Student Affairs Director, Mary Jones. Although pleasant to work with and respected for her programs, Jones had no background in affirmative action. In reality, Mary's presence reduced both the visibility and viability of the affirmative action office. The president would no longer have the political liability of daily confronting new problems uncovered by the office. The new director did not know where to look or what to do if she did uncover something. Restructuring or moving organizational components around was an ongoing process at Stonewall. It was a rational response to effectively heighten control and guarantee predictability.[19] As in the case of the affirmative action office, this made the accomplishment of goals, especially those dealing with change, more difficult.

In a healthy organizational environment, honest discussion of the issues surrounding the Stonewall affirmative action debate would have dissipated the confused and chaotic conditions clouding the issue. Conditions at Stonewall were further exacerbated by a planning process which adroitly excluded information needed to gain insights and make informed decisions about the matter. Power remained in the hands of a few and control was their main way of functioning.[20]

### GROUP BEHAVIOR AND ORGANIZATIONAL CHANGE

An organization is composed of persons and groups related through both its processes and its purposes. For the organization to be strong, the members need to share an established notion of what is correct behavior. It is, however, as a member of a group that the individual is most pliable. The culture and ethos of an organization tend to absorb individuals so that they act not so much by their own value perceptions as by the norms and values comprising the ethics of the organization. If the organizational processes and goals are directed toward change, and for the purposes of this book, pluralism, it is likely that individuals or groups within the organization will work toward and accept change. If, however, the organization's stated goal is pluralism, but the unstated goal, as in the case of Stonewall University, is "Don't rock the boat," the individual and the group are confronted with contradiction, confusion, and ultimately inaction.[21]

During the 1973 Watergate scandal that rocked the Nixon Presidency, group behavior degenerated beyond the organizational imperative of conformity. The deterioration of mental efficiency, reality testing, and moral judgment permeating Nixon's inner circle has since been characterized as "groupthink." Three preconditions increase the likelihood of groupthink in organizations: group cohesiveness, group insulation from "outsiders," and the organizational leaders' promotion of favored solutions. At Stonewall University all three conditions existed over the issue of affirmative action. University personnel found they had to abdicate a part of their conscience to the conscience of the group if they were to continue to be considered "Insiders" and "team players." Belonging to the team required them to take sides on affirmative action even though they might not feel right about the manipulative processes they observed, the scapegoating, and blaming of others.[22] In effect, they had no awareness that there were multiple ways to look at affirmative action, that both sides could be right, and that options existed.

An illusion of invulnerability permeated the institution and helped most of its members to minimize any ethical or moral concerns for their actions toward Smith and the affirmative action program. Believing that shortly the campus would return to "normal," university personnel ignored suggestions that their actions could lead to larger equal opportunity and affirmative action problems. Negative and stereotypical ideas about the program stifled dissent. Each staff member's self-censorship of any deviation from these views reduced the effectiveness or importance of doubts and counterarguments. A shared illusion of unanimity concerning judgments conforming to the majority view underlay administrative actions and policy decisions.

As Chair of the Faculty Senate, Dr. Susan Brown with the president's knowledge, took leadership in blocking Smith's efforts to implement a strong program. Known for her ability to externalize issues and scapegoat innocent victims like the affirmative action officer, Brown was especially effective in opposing reconsideration of the Wing tenure case. Her loyalties lay with a group of faculty known as the Dinosaurs. This group considered the affirmative action program a threat to its power and control of institutional resources. As self-appointed mindguards, the Dinosaurs protected university personnel from information about the program that might shatter complacency about the effectiveness or morality of their actions. At the same time, they developed several strategies to undermine the program. Targeting Smith as the enemy, the Dinosaurs encouraged broad negative judgemental evaluations of his performance. They spread false information about the program. During Faculty Senate meetings, significant information about it was overlooked and sometimes deliberately altered while mundane and insignificant trivia assumed proportions inappropriate to its importance. They encouraged in-fighting between various ethnic cultural groups on campus, raising the existing level of competition for jobs and resources to new heights.

The Dinosaurs embodied Stonewall's unwritten norms and expectations, or world view. They insisted on deciding questions like equality and social justice on their own terms, and organizational rewards, both tangible and intangible, flowed to those adhering to their views. Denying the efficacy or even the legality of federal and state civil rights laws, the Dinosaurs shirked responsibility for their actions through this denial and their ability to control information. By promoting and supporting periodic crises like the affirmative action affair, they were able to excuse and cover up not only their erratic and possibly illegal actions, but also to undermine the university's ability to make long-term plans.[23] Those "Insiders" with reservations about the Dinosaurs' actions remained silent because no norm existed for them to test the appropriateness of those actions. Besides, they knew they had to remain a part of the group in order to keep their jobs. The Dinosaurs could be quite vindictive toward individuals opposing them.

Stonewall University was the entire universe for the Dinosaurs and they viewed every event on the campus as either an assault upon their collective being or an affirmation of their existence. Dishonesty fueled their activities. They lied to themselves, to the people around them, and to the outside world.[24] Many of their distorted views were accepted at face value and given credence by the city's newspapers. Because the affirmative action officer had introduced new ideas into the organization, the Dinosaurs discounted both his experience and his intentions for the program. With the assistance of the Vice President of Academic Affairs and the Faculty Senate Chair, they successfully stonewalled Smith's attempts to implement the affirmative action program. They blocked his appointment to academic committees which had direct relevance to the affirmative action program and refused to invite him to participate in special programs. Similarly, the president chose not to place Smith on his decision-making body, the Executive Cabinet.

Why did other university personnel follow the Dinosaurs' lead and buy into their upside down distortions of the affirmative action program? Why, indeed, when some of these same personnel had been victims of the Dinosaurs' attacks in other encounters? There were some on campus who sensed that maintaining the status quo would not resolve discrimination problems and felt the university needed to address its mission of seeking diversity. They kept their opinions to themselves, probably because they were afraid and felt powerless to challenge the Dinosaurs' illusionary view of reality. Apparently invulnerable to attack, the Dinosaurs appeared to have unanimous support for their views.

Even those who did disagree kept silent, unwilling to risk the Dinosaurs' wrath in order to bring the organization into congruence with its own mission and purpose. Instead they followed the Dinosaurs' lead in rallying to the president's defense when "Outsiders" questioned the removal of Smith from his office. They went along with the Dinosaurs' rigid condemnation of the affirmative action program and insistence that traditional institutional norms and habits provide solutions to any problems on the campus.

Employees knew their continued membership in the Stonewall University "family" depended on adhering to the rigid rules and established norms championed by the Dinosaurs. Loyalty to the university in effect had become a substitute for their own lives and for remaining true to what they believed was the right thing to do.[25] In healthy organizations, members confront the issues because their sense of self-worth emanates from doing what they know is right rather than merely being liked or a part of the team. In these organizations, employees' ideas, conflicts, and reactions are "a rich source of continual change."[26] At Stonewall University, employees went to great lengths to avoid open conflict and difficult issues. The institution had a high turnover rate outside faculty ranks. People were always leaving and new ones arriving to take their places. Like cogs in a machine, these new employees bought into the confused communication processes of the organization, fueled by secrets and gossip. The systemic defensive routine remained intact. It was usually described to these new employees as the "Stonewall way of doing things."

## CAN ORGANIZATIONS CHANGE?

Can unhealthy organizations like Stonewall University change to accept new paradigms? Can they actually deal with the changes in workforce patterns now taking place in American society? For years social scientists have sought to answer the first question, and it is fair to say that most of their experiments came from the realization that something is often not right with how people are integrated or treated in organizations. So far the applied work of the behavioral sciences has mainly served to patch up holes in the existing organizational fabric rather than focusing on the philosophical root of the problem. Authors Schaef and Fassel offer one answer. They propose treating the problem, not the symptoms, and simultaneously focusing on the organizational processes, "the structures, the product, and the procedures."[27]

Throughout this book we have equated development of an organizational personality to the development of human behavior. If humans can change negative traits, so can organizations. The change process, however, must start with the recognition that there is a problem and this recognition must emanate from the top of the organization. Executive leadership is essential if change is to happen. Organizational behaviorist Ken Blanchard's model of change has relevance to this discussion of organizational personality change. He identifies four levels leading to change:

- KNOWLEDGE: Easy to change by reading or training.
- ATTITUDE: Emotional reaction to knowledge can be positive or negative.
- INDIVIDUAL BEHAVIOR: Change in attitude to reach this level must occur (the longer the person is engaged in a behavior, the harder it is to change that behavior).
- ORGANIZA-TIONAL BEHAVIOR: The most difficult level of change and executives must attain previous levels before organizational change can occur.[28]

Today, affirmative action in dysfunctional organizations seldom goes beyond the information stage. Although strong emotional reactions to affirmative action normally occur at the individual level, the organization operating dysfunctionally will seldom probe into these reactions. In the case of Stonewall University, there is clearly lack of recognition of a problem, emotions are running high, everything is secretive and closed in denial. As you read the rest of this book, continue to ask yourself where is my organization in the change process and how ready is it for Workforce 2000?

Dysfunctional organizations must recognize their unhealthy symptoms if they are to deal with their problems:

- Loss of organizational memory
- Replication of old patterns and old solutions
- Search for the "Quick Fix"
- Reinforcement of the organizational imperative
- Evidence of "Group Think"
- Resorting to scapegoating and blaming others
- Adoption of the "good guys" versus the "bad guys" syndrome
- Existence of a vague, confused, and ineffective communication system
- Distortion and manipulation of the truth

- Secrecy and denial
- Isolation from reality which breeds the "Insiders" versus "Outsiders" syndrome
- Self-centeredness
- Crisis orientation
- Use of planning as a form of control
- Verbalization of commitment toward change while maintaining the status quo

Can unhealthy organizational personalities actually deal with demographic changes now taking place in American society and the workplace? The answer is yes if first they recognize they have a problem and secondly they deal with their negative internal values. Also, as change takes place, dysfunctional organizations need to carefully avoid trading one set of problems for another set, for example replacing the "Loser's Syndrome" mentality with the "Winner's Syndrome." Chapter Five presents a diagnostic model for changing the organizational personality. Before that, however, in Chapter Four we examine current organizational behavior and its effect on diversity and discrimination issues through several individual and group case studies.

# CHAPTER 4
## Outsiders Inside The Old Paradigm

INTRODUCTION

The long-awaited "glass ceiling" report of the United States Department of Labor was finally unveiled in August 1991. This review of nine Fortune 500 companies receiving federal contracts revealed widespread intentional and unintentional practices which prevented women and minorities from advancing into middle- and upper-level management. Following the release of the report, Labor Secretary Lynn Martin held a press conference wherein she "promised to help U. S. corporations shatter the 'glass ceiling' that keeps minorities and women from advancing." Asserting that "the progress of these groups in corporate America was affected by more than just qualifications and career choices," Martin also pledged to use her position as a "bully pulpit to encourage every corporation to develop its own strategy for promoting women and minorities."[1]

Many of the report's findings underlined the prevalence of old paradigm barriers and the ineffectiveness of affirmative action programs. For instance, although the organizational structures, cultures, business sectors, and personnel policies differed widely among the nine companies studied, common characteristics existed relating to stereotypes and misperceptions about equal opportunity and affirmative action. These included:

- a lack of integration of equal opportunity principles into developmental programs and policies for the advancement of women and minorities, especially at the higher levels of the corporate ladder;

- a failure to monitor appraisal and compensation systems
  and review total compensation packages to ensure nondiscrimination;
- an absence of minorities and women at the highest levels of
  management and, if present, almost always in staff functions;
- a deficiency in record-keeping systems for recruitment, employment, and developmental activities for management-type
  positions.[2]

The study identified organizational recruitment practices as
some of the significant reasons why minorities and women did not
advance further in corporate America. Such practices included
word-of-mouth recruitment, employee referrals, and corporate use
of executive search and referral firms which were unaware of
affirmative action and equal employment opportunity requirements. Other conditions creating the "glass ceiling" were lack of
opportunity for women and minorities to contribute to, and participate in, corporate developmental programs and a general lack
of understanding in the company that equal employment opportunity is not one person's responsibility. It was particularly noted
that the EEO director actively participated in the filling of vacancies
below the management levels and that managers at the entry-level
were often given training and made aware of equal employment
opportunity and affirmative action concerns. However, as managers moved up the corporate ladder to senior-level positions where
key decisions were made, there was a general lack of continued
awareness building or reaffirmation of corporate values regarding
equal employment opportunity and equal access.[3]

The report affirmed the Labor Department's support for equal
employment opportunity and affirmative action in all aspects of
employment throughout the workplace as well as the personal
involvement of chief executive officers. It also recognized the
importance of corporate culture in the implementation of effective
equal employment opportunity and affirmative action programs
and the need for increased executive responsibility for cultural
changes at every level through creative incentive compensation
plans.

Martin vowed she would not try to smash the "glass ceiling"
with what she called a "500-pound hammer" by refusing to give
government contracts to corporations that overtly or covertly bar

women and minorities from reaching the top. But she did outline a four-point program that called for: 1. further review of the nine companies in question; 2. internal education of Labor Department officials on the "glass-ceiling" issue; 3. a public awareness campaign to encourage voluntary improvements by companies; and 4. an award program for businesses that take effective steps to encourage equal opportunity.[4]

Although documenting what we already know and have known for years, the "glass-ceiling" report signaled that our national leaders are now publicly recognizing something is not right out there. But it did not answer one central question. Will Martin's statements just become part of the existing social myth and perpetuate the view that our national political leaders believe in diversity while their actions belie their statements? Or will they actually begin the shift towards new paradigm thinking?

In the preceding chapters we have discussed problems like the "glass-ceiling" which are perpetuated by the old paradigm and how dysfunctional organizational personalities can exacerbate problems faced by Workforce 2000 groups. We have made the point that organizational cultures must change if they are to meet the Workforce 2000 challenge. Many organizations, as documented in the Department of Labor study, continue to provide fertile soil for perpetuation of exclusionary behaviors toward individuals and groups comprising Workforce 2000. Those affected, however, are not only the minorities and females cited in the report, but older and disabled workers as well. Although there is much that seems bleak on the employment horizon, there are some bright spots in the organizational landscape. In Secretary of Labor Martin's words there are companies, each of which is working to "develop its own strategy" for making the transition into a new paradigm. One of these is the Walgreens Company. Later in this chapter we will look at some of its programs.

In this chapter we also examine the effect of organizational behaviors on an individual through the Barbara Jenkins case and on groups through the Tucson Police Department *Cota and Falls, et al v. City of Tucson* lawsuit. In each case the specific problems of the old paradigm and the resultant organizational inability to hear voices of change in the environment exacerbate existing problems. The result is lost resources and opportunities for both employer and employee.

## 1. BARBARA JENKINS

Barbara Jenkins is a woman of color who has held management positions in large private sector organizations for fifteen years. She exhibits all the signs of an individual who is about to "drop out" of the organization. Joseph Raelin calls this behavior maladaptive in "Clash of Cultures."[5] Whatever term you use, the constant stress of being on the outside of a culture has affected her ability to self-actualize. Although others see her as successful, she is constantly reminded by the people around her that her success is not due to her skills but to her race and/or her sex. It is very possible that at some point, men of color will gain acceptance because of their sex and white females may gain acceptance because of their race. The woman of color, however, may experience more discrimination, sometimes for race, sometimes for sex, and sometimes for both.

"Starting with my very first position, I remember by mentor saying, 'Here's what you need to do to fit in.' Every time I hear that statement, I can't help wondering 'what's wrong with me'? Over the years I have changed a lot. Somewhere there is still some of the real me left but I have to cling to her with all my might! There are days when I think that she and I are clutching hands over a cliff, she starts to slip away, and I can see the terror in her eyes. All I can do is tell her to hold on.

"On my first assignment, eager to please, I soaked up everything that I was told, changing from caterpillar to butterfly, working long hours and sacrificing my personal life for a chance to grab the brass ring. The company rewarded me with several promotions for my contributions and this made me a 'first' in several areas. I've blocked out, like I do with anything painful, what precipitated the following conversation, but one day I remarked to my supervisor's manager about how hard I had worked to attain my current status. He said, 'That had nothing to do with it, we made you and don't you forget it.' This conversation took place at the height of the Civil Rights Movement and it never dawned on me that my progress was due to something other than my own talents. At first I was bewildered by his remark. After all, I could, if necessary, show visible proof of changes (improving our operations) which were incorporated because of my ideas — changes which had been adopted by my peers as the standard. I could also point to other nonminority employees promoted at a similar rate whose track record did not equal mine, and for whom I had often been asked to clean up the messes they had created. I walked away from the encounter hurt and angry. Little did I know that this scenario would be repeated throughout my career.

"Maybe that's why there is an ache and pain that touches deep in my soul every time I'm promoted. My excitement is always short-lived as I wait for the inevitable comment that I was only promoted because I am black and/or female and not because of my talents and expertise. I'm still not sure why I bother to work so hard. It must be my father's influence 'always do the very best you can, you are lucky to be where you are, don't ever forget that.'

"I guess I'm holding out for what seems like the impossible — being valued for my contributions and not for my race or my sex. You've heard that song, 'Fifty Ways to Lose Your Lover?' Well, I think I've learned 'Fifty Ways to Tell a Minority They Just Don't Quite Fit.' I've started to refer to this as the 'moving finish line.' No matter what you do, you can never quite get there. If I'm quiet and reserved, I'm not aggressive enough. If I become more aggressive, I'm not a team player or I'm too threatening. If I'm assertive, I'm too impatient. If I speak up, I'm too intelligent which translates to a know-it-all. If I keep quiet, I'm either stupid or angry.

"Additional credentials don't seem to help. My academic credentials are first-rate, yet I can still speak from my area of expertise and have my suggestions ignored. Often the person to whom I make the recommendations will decide to proceed with them after asking someone else about them and receiving their confirmation that they are good ideas. I can never quite figure out why they can't hear me when I say the same things. Of course, I can rationalize that it doesn't matter what these other people think as long as I know the truth, but it does! Especially if those other people make decisions which affect my life.

"You see, I want to have a real 'win' where I can experience that exhilaration that goes with winning. I want to know what a major league champion feels when he goes out on the field and wins the big one. I watch the World Series and the Super Bowl and wonder what that emotion is all about.

"When you ask me if I have worked in any dysfunctional organizations and what impact they've had on me, it's difficult to point to any one thing. I can say that I have experienced a great deal of emotional pain during what some people would call an extremely successful career. I can also say that in moving around in an attempt to control my own destiny, I have gained broad business knowledge that I'm sure I would have missed if I had remained in one place, so out of chaos comes some rewards.

"I can look back and see friends who stayed with previous employers who were far more qualified than I and most have yet to achieve the level of responsibility of which I know they are capable. I do believe my experience in business is worth all the moves and the pain. I equate it to someone who goes to Europe and only stays in France. You see, my career is like going to Europe and visiting France, Germany, Italy, and out-of-the-way cities that no one ever heard of. Because of this, I believe that one day someone will need an expert with unique skills and my name will be mentioned — not because I'm Black and/or female, but because I'm the best. Maybe then I can have my Super Bowl celebration."

Barbara has not resolved the incongruence between her personal values and her professional life in dysfunctional organizations. Barbara's father gave her a "work hard and you will achieve" work ethic, but everything she has experienced tells her all her co-workers and peers see is her race and sex, not her work ethic or achievements. Her many moves have caused her to acquire a new value set with every new group in order to "fit." By her own admission she may be in danger of losing sight of the "real" person. In the interview, during a discussion of her high school days, she mentioned that she enjoyed acting and had ambitions to be an actress at one time. When pressed about whether she ever regretted not pursuing an acting career, she looked up, stared for a minute and replied, "I am acting every day. Some days I'm just better at it than others."

Barbara's interview revealed that in order to advance her career, she chose to work in successful organizations that were in a mature market stage (Winner's Syndrome) or financially distressed groups (Loser's Syndrome) that needed "turnaround" management skills. Both of these types of organizations may have cultures steeped in the old paradigm and resistant to change as discussed in Chapter Two. Barbara will continue to experience job stress until she finds an organization with different role expectations or she develops a more suitable method of accommodating the conflict between her values and the values of the group. We believe she will quit and "drop out" of corporate America.

Like Barbara, individuals throughout the United States "survive" their jobs in organizations by psyching themselves down to go to work each day. They lob off big parts of their minds, spirit, and souls to go in and do a job where they feel unwanted, unappreciated, and dismissed. Dismissal is the appropriate term for the Tucson Police Department case which follows. The department's historic disregard of Spanish language use has led to a major lawsuit. At the core of this suit is the Police Department's reluctance to respond to a culturally and linguistically diverse community.

## 2. THE TUCSON POLICE DEPARTMENT CASE

Language is a window on cultural values. How the dominant culture treats language differences can validate a culture or sub-culture or can obscure that group's value to society. Because language cannot be separated from a group's identity, it has been used like skin color, sex, disability, and age in the United States to distinguish between those traditionally on the inside and those on the outside of organizational life. Only now are we as a nation beginning to recognize the implications and positive impact of language differences in our workplaces and the increasing need to use language as a business tool in the larger world economy.

Although an official language or monolingualism has never existed in the United States, anti-foreigner or nativist sentiments and attempts to limit the usage of languages other than English have existed throughout our history.[6] In Tucson, Arizona, where many residents reside whose native tongue is not English, the tensions over language valuation have strong historic foundations reaching back to 1854 when the Gadsden Purchase brought the city into the United States. Recently these tensions erupted in a major lawsuit involving the Tucson Police Department. That court action brings into focus the implications of language differences in a changing workforce.

Language discrimination in the police department was for-mally raised in 1980 by the Mexican-American Police Officers' Association, and subsequently the City's affirmative action office investigated the complaint. Their report recommended that the police department recognize the usefulness of bilingual skills, conduct tests to ascertain the levels of Spanish language profi-ciency among its personnel, and implement a pay increase for those who met certification requirements. Despite continued em-ployee complaints, these recommendations were not implemented.

Although cognizant of the need to interact effectively with a substantial Spanish-speaking population, the Tucson Police Department continued to try to meet these needs through a set of informal ad hoc practices. Hispanic officers and staff personnel increasingly noted that these practices placed a disproportionate burden on them by adding significantly to their workload and responsibilities. In addition, departmental policy requiring the use of Spanish and failure to use bilingual skills as a basis for disciplinary action further exacerbated the problem. Because of this policy, Hispanic employees with a low level of Spanish proficiency also reported high levels of stress and anxiety. At the same time, those employees with a higher level of Spanish proficiency, because of the heavier workloads, objected to assuming the work responsibilities of others not possessing language skills.[7]

Apparently, the departmental assumption was that all Hispanics spoke Spanish and possessed sufficient skills to serve the complex responsibility of police work. In reality this simply was not the case. According to the plaintiff's attorney, Richard Martinez, eighty percent of those Hispanic officers listed as bilingual and required to conduct intricate work in Spanish felt they lacked the skills to do so on a consistent basis. As a practical matter they were subjected to different terms and conditions of employment from monolingual English speakers in the department.[8]

Compounding the problem was the failure of the City of Tucson's Human Resource Department to develop policies which took into account Spanish language skills in recruitment, selection, and training of police department personnel. A study of the demand for Spanish language services on the department and the effect of these demands on employees' job performance coupled with the implementation of policies designed to take into account those requirements would have relieved existing tensions. Such policies are becoming increasingly common in both the public and private sector where multilingual environments exist.

A broad range of options exist for employers like the City of Tucson needing to maintain language competent services. For example, they could try to make a valid and objective identification of existing employee abilities and the scope and depth of their competence. Employers could also provide for the requirement of competency, where appropriate, in job specifications, education and training programs, and in the development of staffing and compensation policies. Such actions eliminate the effect of assumptions about language use. They also deal with the failure to recognize the use of bilingual personnel such as that occurring in the City of Tucson. In the process, potential threats of employees challenging such treatment as discriminatory are dispelled.[9]

When the Tucson Police Department case actually went to trial, tensions escalated within the department and drew the attention of both elected officials and the media. Accusations of harassment of Hispanic police officers and police staff surfaced, and fears grew that such behavior jeopardized both officer and citizen safety.[10]

There is no denying that the City of Tucson's inability to "hear" about bilingual needs and capabilities has been costly in terms of resources, productivity, and departmental effectiveness. On a broader level, however, this lawsuit will raise public consciousness about language issues — one of a myriad of questions facing employers as the country races toward the Twenty-First Century. The suit also signals to employers continuing to operate in the old paradigm that they face increasingly hard choices. Whether dealing with sexual harassment which questions the very way the sexes have traditionally interacted in the workplace, or the prevailing stereotypes about older employees and their cost to the organization, or the provision of workplace accommodations for disabled Americans, old paradigm managers face a clear message: a paradigm shift is occurring in the workplace, and they need to change as well.

## 3. TRANSITIONS: THE WALGREENS EXAMPLE

As one of the organizations implementing programs to deal with changing workforce and customer dynamics in the United States, Walgreens is looking to the future with a healthy respect for long-range results. Nearly a century ago, the company's founder, Charles R. Walgreen Sr., planted the seeds for keeping Walgreens' eyes on environmental change. His emphasis on the importance of Walgreens' customers guided the growth of the pioneer company in pharmaceuticals and retail services from a single drug store on Chicago's South Side in 1901 to a nationwide chain of nearly 1,700 stores today. "Every customer is a guest in our store and should be treated as such. . . . It is unusual service, uncommon thoughtfulness that makes customers remember a store, brings them back, leads them to speak favorably of it to others."[11]

When acknowledging the 1985 Dun's Business Month award as one of the nation's five best managed companies, Walgreens' President C. R. Walgreen III demonstrated in words the effect of the founder's vision on the company. "Walgreens is not 36,000 people serving more than a million customers a day," he stated, "it's one employee serving one customer in one store. The way we do that today and tomorrow will determine whether we can stay at the top of our industry."[12]

Walgreens has moved beyond understanding the importance of "hearing" the customers of tomorrow and employment of a workforce which will serve the needs of these customers. It has begun to implement organization-wide programs like its "Valuing and Managing Diversity" course designed to help supervisors and managers transcend cultural and communication barriers. Within the next three years all of the company's supervisors and managers will attend the course to gain an understanding of how to work in cooperation with those whose values, priorities, and feelings may be different from their own.[13]

Programs unique to one part of the country are another way Walgreens is taking steps to deal with changing workplace and customer demographics. In Miami, Florida, for example, Spanish language commercials are being produced especially for the local market. Translated commercials have been a Walgreens' staple for years. The Miami commercials, however, are created exclusively for a local Hispanic market. Through them the company lets the community know they have Hispanic employees at all levels, that the employees speak Spanish and understand the Hispanic customer. The commercials were filmed in Miami's new Bird Road Walgreens where bilingual signs were printed for holiday promotions and where every sign is bilingual — wall decals, aisle markers, and plastic cornice inserts. While the company acknowledges the challenge of finding merchandise to appeal to the diverse Hispanic market because what may appeal to Cubans in Miami may not sell to Mexicans in San Antonio, it is already casting its eyes to an equally diverse and growing U. S. Asian market.[14]

The company is also developing programs to respond to the needs of different groups comprising its workforce. In Tucson, Arizona, District Manager Mort Grayam has implemented a unique program known as "fair scheduling." The traditionally unfavorable shifts (nights, holidays, weekends) have been spread throughout all workers' schedules, and each employee now has a fair shot at more favorable shifts. Employees are allowed to write their own schedules which are then submitted to management. Final schedules are established through consensus, with management stepping in only when consensus cannot be reached.

When the "fair scheduling" program was implemented, there were several employees with seniority who enjoyed the advantage of selecting the "best" hours to work. Although the program did not benefit them personally, they found it increased both the efficiency and productivity of their departments.[15] At corporate headquarters in Chicago, Illinois, a new approach to pregnancy leave has been developed. It began when an employee learned she was expecting twins and her physician advised her to work at home during the last months of her pregnancy. Walgreens accommodated with a computer, phone line hookup, an MCI card for business calls, and programs which she could perform from her home base.[16]

As Tucson District Manager, Mort Grayam, explains, "It's always nice to be ahead of the law," and in many areas the company appears to have been ahead of it for years. It was the first chain drug company in the state of Louisiana to hire an African-American pharmacist in 1963. Today one of its regional managers and vice presidents is African-American. Although vice presidents are still mandated to retire at age 65, the company has many older employees like District Manager Tony Sgarlatti who continues an active worklife at seventy-four years of age.[17]

Until recently Walgreens' approach to disability issues was a grass roots effort, but now corporate headquarters has instituted a program to deal with disabled access to job opportunities and to develop staff training. One grass roots project initiated with the Arizona School for the Deaf and the Blind (ASDB) offers students the chance to work in Walgreens stores for a few hours a week. Through part-time work, these students gain self-confidence and their first job experience. At the same time, managers discover a new source of ideas for customer relations and a potential employee pool of conscientious and reliable workers. Jorge Figueroa, a hearing-impaired student, first worked for Walgreens while at ASDB and has since moved to a full-time job with the company. He rotates through three Walgreens stores as an inventory/pricing clerk and "plans to work for Walgreens for a long time."[18]

CONCLUSION

Strategically, Walgreens recognizes the nationwide demographic shift signaling customer and workforce change and it is taking the first transitional steps toward a new paradigm. In the process the company is also benefiting from listening to the voices of change. In Chapter Five we expand further on the healthy organizational response to Workforce 2000 issues by looking at *The Miami Herald* experience. We also present a diagnostic model which should help organizations identify how to recognize their needs and solve their problems as they move toward the new paradigm.

# CHAPTER 5
## Toward A New Paradigm

INTRODUCTION

The glass ceiling, where it exists, hinders not only individuals but society as a whole. It effectively cuts our pool of potential corporate leaders by eliminating over one-half of our population. It deprives our economy of new leaders, new sources of creativity — the "would be" pioneers of the business world. If our end game is to compete successfully in today's global market, then we have to unleash the full potential of the American Workforce. The time has come to tear down, to dismantle — the "Glass Ceiling."[1]

These words from "A Report on the Glass Ceiling Initiative" give compelling reasons for the new paradigm. Increasingly the reality is that the United States' role as the prime decision-maker in today's global society is rapidly declining. The reversal of this pattern requires a vision beyond world dominance. Elimination of the old paradigm and its concomitant organizational myth is essential if future generations are to continue to live the American dream. In order to achieve that goal it is necessary to understand what the organizational myth is and how the sociotechnical approach to organizational change can eliminate it. It is also vital to recognize that central to the process of change is enlightened organizational leadership as illustrated by the case of *The Miami Herald* newspaper.

1. THE ORGANIZATIONAL MYTH

Like the social myth, the organizational myth is a fictional version of reality which can serve as a determinant of how a society, or a part of society, behaves. It can serve as a positive force, as in the belief that good is rewarded and evil is inevitably punished, or as a negative force, as in Adolf Hitler's Great Lie that all Germany's problems after World War I stemmed from conspirators. George Sorel in *Reflections on Violence* popularized the social myth as a belief based on fiction to manipulate a segment of society to take violent action when the leader called for a workers' revolution against capitalism. For Sorel, it did not matter whether the myth was based on the truth or not as long as it was effective in influencing people to act in a certain way.

Like the social myth, the organizational myth can serve as a positive force, as in stories of an organization's origin providing inspiration to its personnel, or as a negative force as in the Stonewall University case. Publicly the university proclaimed its support for multicultural and diversity objectives when in reality its unstated goal was to subvert pluralism. Like the root of organizational personalities, organizational myths grow from the seeds planted by the founder or founders of the group. They reflect the values programmed into the organization that have shaped its direction and attitudes over time. Too often organizational myths reflecting old paradigm thinking (social generalizations, the illusion of organizational rationality, and the organizational imperative) negatively affect the future participants in Workforce 2000. This is particularly true of dysfunctional organizations where organizational myths are particularly destructive. For instance, in the Stonewall case, Dr. Heine "Dutch" Heineken espoused a belief in diversity while simultaneously undercutting programs to assimilate Workforce 2000 participants. As a newly appointed president he was severely chided by local women's groups about sexist comments made during a speech about female faculty. Women greeted his seemingly sincere plea to be judged on his actions and not his words with skepticism, but chose not to press the issue. It should come as little surprise that the number of female faculty dramatically declined during his tenure. What actually occurred under his leadership became the mirror reflecting his true beliefs.

A key indicator of an organization's response to diversity issues is the presence of the negative organizational myth. While leaders and groups within the organization perpetuate a public image of support for diversity, in reality internal values ensure that old paradigm rules prevail. Through manipulation of statistics, rules and regulations, and individuals, these organizations maintain a pseudo image of change. In such organizations the myth flourishes in an environment of denial and secrecy to escape or mask the real problem. Newcomers to the organization innocently identifying problems are encouraged to conform to "our way" or to leave.

## 2. I'M O.K., YOU'RE O.K.

Organizational leaders can look back to the 1960s and the faddish expression, "I'm o.k., You're o.k.,"[2] to find the genesis of the 1990s denial syndrome blocking change in organizations and perpetuating the negative organizational myth. Today many organizations through old paradigm behavior assume the role of the "excluding adult" devoid of the charm, spontaneity, and fun which are characteristic of the healthy child. At the same time, they reject the adult functions of reevaluating old data in order to have the freedom to change and respond to new stimuli in new ways. Operating in an illusion of rationality and objectivity, they perpetuate the negative organizational myth. The myth in turn excludes diversity.

The sociotechnical approach facilitates organization action shifts calculated to eliminate negative organizational myths. This approach takes organizations beyond the first stage of change — knowledge — and assists them in identifying and resolving their dysfunctional characteristics. With this model, the focus is on the group rather than the individual.

## 3. WHAT PEOPLE DO IS A SUM OF WHAT THEY KNOW

Organizations, like their leaders, are the sum of what they know. Many organizations, especially dysfunctional ones, fail to utilize environmental information. The following quotation from *Outlook Magazine* highlights this point:

American education has always failed sizable segments of the population, particularly women and minorities. The needs of the workforce have changed, but our schools continue to accomplish what they were designed to do: ensure the success of white males. Until the system is redesigned to meet the needs of all of our children in this multicultural society, it will continue to fail.[3]

If the school system is structured to mirror society and managing diversity was not part of the curriculum for our current leaders, where will they learn this new style of management? Leaders growing up with certain stereotypical ideas about minorities, women, the disabled, or the aged, are caught between their perceptions and the realities of tomorrow's workforce. According to Thomas Kuhn's *The Structure of Scientific Revolutions*, scientists learn new processes, not by study, but by actual experience. Observing and participating in applying concepts to solutions is the only answer.[4] We believe this is also true for diversity. As in the "Winner's Syndrome" and the "Loser's Syndrome," the major impediment, in Kuhn's definition of the learning process, is the individual ceasing to learn on a continuous basis. The resulting limited field of vision leads to the discounting of valuable information, people, and ideas as irrelevant or useless in the decision-making and/or problem-solving process.

Several models to deal with change have emerged within the last two decades. Keith Davis in *Behavior at Work* suggests three common methods organizations use today to initiate change. The most popular method is to alter the environmental forces affecting employees. Alterations might involve initiating better leadership, changing the formal organization, or receiving new pressures from the informal organization. Individuals' perceptions of the forces surrounding them are altered in the second method, what Davis calls "improved communication." A third method is to alter the basic value system of one or more persons involved in the change through sensitivity training or psychological counseling.[5] Each method focuses on the individual as part of a group, not on the group itself, and assumes rational, healthy organizations.

But in order to address the needs of a diverse workforce in a dysfunctional organization, change programs must focus on the group. It is true that groups consist of individuals, but it is the collective personality of the group which brings strong pressure upon its members to change.[6] By utilizing the sociotechnical model, organizations can uncover the historical imprinting on its internal structures and systems currently affecting its decision-making processes. This model also helps the organization to develop the data needed to facilitate change.

Since dysfunctional groups are blind to their negative traits and the impact of these traits on organizational performance, new employees or individuals with backgrounds different from the primary group are particularly valuable during the data collecting stage. These individuals are more likely to "see" what the organization calls "normal" as "abnormal." That can prove invaluable in the development of action plans for removal of dysfunctional group behaviors. In short the sociotechnical process reveals what the organization knows. By assigning this data to one of two categories, "inherent" (a change in values), or "specific cause effect" (the result of values), one can derive a knowledge base for action plans. This plan can then be utilized to train and/or communicate the new paradigm — the new vision — to the organization.

Through use of the sociotechnical model, the organization will address the three basic results called for in "A Report on the Glass Ceiling Initiative":

- Identification of systemic barriers to the career development of minorities and women;
- Elimination of those barriers through corrective and cooperative problem-solving; and
- Furthering the departments' and the employer community's understanding of how to identify and eliminate discriminatory and artificial barriers.[7]

## 4. THE SOCIOTECHNICAL MODEL

The sociotechnical approach (Figure 1) focuses simultaneously on the organization's technical and social systems and assists in diagnosing the impact of group values on the change process. Recognized as the key to the success of Japanese corporations, the sociotechnical approach incorporates the relationship existing in all organizations, the balance between people or social systems and the technical system.[8] It is the social system that usually reveals the negative attributes of a dysfunctional organization. It is the positive energy, the synergy, between the various systems in the sociotechnical model that provides the critical element for creation of the new paradigm.[9] Although the organization's future technical systems may remain unchanged, it is unlikely that the supporting social infrastructure will escape adjustment to new realities. Rather than viewing the validity of Workforce 2000 demographic shifts as a threat, organizations can use this opportunity to review historical practices in search of obsolete

Figure 1:
Sociotechnical Framework
Five Key Inputs

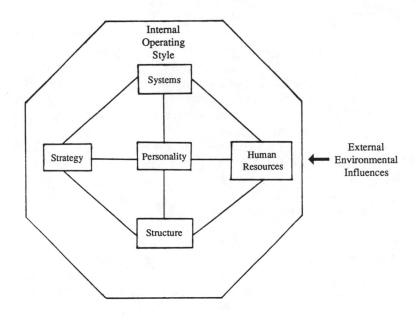

Modified from the original sociotechnical model by Professor Robert R. Rehder, University of New Mexico.

patterns obstructing change. Without such a review, even the most current technical systems will continue to fail in dysfunctional organizations.

The proposed model will assist in identifying the key characteristics of an organization's personality and the effect of social systems on technical systems. In turn, the corresponding changes will become the foundation for a plan unique to organizational needs and the relationship of diversity to actual accomplishment of the plan. This approach improves the organization's ability to identify the effects of external influences on internal operating procedures.

Reviewing and evaluating the five key elements (systems, strategy, structure, human resources, and personality) in the sociotechnical model enables the organization to identify those elements which contribute most to its adaptability to new workforce needs. Take, for example, the common organizational personality types identified in Chapter Two: the "Winner's Syndrome," the "Loser's Syndrome," and the "Quick Fix." The "Winner's Syndrome," based on the right way to approach such matters as markets and product development, indicates a strong influence of strategy and systems. "Winner's Syndrome" organizations are the most susceptible to external forces. Usually leaders in their markets, they are accustomed to setting trends, not following them. Their leadership position indicates a strong human resource element that executes strategy and develops systems effectively. Environmental change, however, dictates a change in strategy. Imagine a winning professional football team's offense suddenly being told to play defense. Although this is an extreme example, it is representative of the fate of a group operating in a new game with old rules. Without a complete change in strategy, plans, and sometimes players, this group will fail. Organizations exhibiting the "Winner's Syndrome" are in the same situation. If organizations in this category have not digressed to the "Loser's Syndrome," and if they have a clear vision and direction, they will usually not need to address structure unless it improves their ability to address strategy. For "Winner's Syndrome" organizations, a revised strategy is the appropriate order of change.

On the other hand, the classical dysfunctional organization exhibiting the "Loser's Syndrome" is usually in a negative financial or market position. This group typically attempts to address strategy first, when in reality it is the human resource element that will have the greatest effect on turning the organization around. Organizations with the "Loser's Syndrome" generally have a cynical workforce wasting valuable time and energy "looking for the hidden meaning." With this group, even a well-defined strategy can be misinterpreted or poorly implemented as power brokers jockey for position or sabotage the efforts of others. Here structural changes are needed. They will work most effectively if leaders in pivotal functions and willing to challenge the status quo are left in place for more than two years.

"Quick Fix" groups suffer from a lack of creative problem-solving skills. Their solutions tend to be faddish and lack long-term effect. Alteration in personality for this group is achieved through changes in systems and procedures. Internal operating processes which are clearly linked to evaluation systems and execution of goals and objectives is required to eliminate quick fix solutions. A system that monitors progress provides an even bigger payoff. It also discourages the short-term quick fix employee who is especially adept at moving on before the bomb explodes.

## 5. ORGANIZATIONAL LEADERSHIP: THE MIAMI HERALD CASE

In addressing old paradigm problems the management of healthy organizations consistently displays three key characteristics: leadership, vision, and direction. David Lawrence, publisher of *The Miami Herald*, clearly understands the significance of all three. From the moment you meet him, you sense there is something special about him. His words are rapid fire, honed by years of developing his views as he speaks about pluralism. Although Lawrence has a definite "presence," it is not his appearance but his words that command attention.

**"I started my career working at a succession of newspapers, and probably would be classified traditionally as a Liberal, although I don't even like the term anymore. Although I have done a fair amount of public speaking on the issues of diversity, it's only been in the last twenty years that I have honed my thinking on the subject. I was raised on a farm in upstate New York in a town with only one black family. Clearly one black family or one outside family of any sort couldn't be a threat to anybody so, logically enough, there wasn't any racial conflict when I was**

growing up. In 1956 when I was 14, our family moved to Florida. The Supreme Court decision that would set the tone for civil rights in the next several decades had already occurred, but still was not in the consciousness of most Americans. During the time I was in high school, the sheriff of my county (and sheriffs traditionally had lots of power in Florida) literally led the KKK through the black section of town. If I know anything from my heritage, it is my parents taught us to be fair. I am not saying that we were America's most progressive family, and we certainly weren't America's most liberal family, but it was a family that had some sense of how you treat people fairly."[10]

The young David Lawrence was aware that many things were happening around him that were inconsistent with the values of fairness passed on to him by his family. Similarly new paradigm organizations have discerned the incongruence between the ideal of diversity and unfair bureaucratic practices that exclude large portions of America's population. Perhaps these organizations were founded during a time when Workforce 2000 participants were not an integral part of an organization's development. However, through leadership and management of the organizational value systems, these new paradigm institutions are consciously seeking a consistent and fair approach to human resources management. Lawrence's background and experience as editor and publisher at several newspapers philosophically prepared him to take this type of leadership role at *The Miami Herald*. He knows there is more than one way to accomplish organizational objectives.

"We went through a whole five-year strategic planning exercise last year and the process of the last two months was based on a strategic vision for the newspaper. We spent a full day talking solely about what the mission and priorities of these newspapers should be. The result is this mission statement:

To publish newspapers which serve our community with excellence vigilance, truthfulness, fairness, and compassion. To foster a sense of community among diverse groups to be essential to those whom we strive to serve, our readers and advertisers, and be editorially independent and financially strong.

"There are seven goals required to accomplish this mission one of which is to have a productive, challenged, diverse workforce. I do not personally use the term affirmative action; I don't like the term, and I steer away from it. In my view it is a 'governmental' word that has come to be seen by some people as the opposite of fairness. So when you start using terms like affirmative action, eyes glaze over and it absolutely ends any intelligent discussion. Fairness means as much to me as anything does and, in fact, my philosophy of pluralism is based on my philosophy of fairness. If you had to ask what words I'd hope you'd put on my tombstone, it would be, 'HE TRIED TO BE FAIR.' I'm trying to make some incremental progress that makes a stronger foundation that somebody else can pick up, progress secure enough that you can't roll back the times. I realize that my definition of fair might differ from somebody else's. I do have some ability to listen to people who disagree with me, and not be particularly offended by it. A newspaper ought to have lots of room for lots of people with lots of different opinions. So what I try to be is 'fair.' I do not claim that we have approached true nirvana or even truth. What I hope we do is impress people enough over time for them to say, 'Yeah, they certainly aren't error-free, but they care about being fair, they try to get the facts right, and they care about this community.'

"Frankly, the problem is how do I get people to hold that vision in their souls over time? The way my vision gets transmitted first to people, not because I intend it that way, is that people will say, 'Aha, the next slot is for an "X." ' So I am constantly trying to work around here to make sure that people don't say that because I don't believe it's true and it is downright perilous for that kind of racial politics to exist. I've seen it happen time and time again; if a minority hires another minority for a key slot, there will be a wave of rumbling in the newsroom about, 'Oh, I see they hired one of their own.' Now a white city editor can hire a white person and they'll say, 'Oh, he's just working on the standard.'

"So the only way that I know to get to the future is to know that you are going to have a lot of that kind of talk and that the only way to deal with it is to simply deal with it — know it's part of the price and ultimately you build a stronger foundation of people who forget that it was ever any different.

"In the process of looking at ourselves again strategically, diversity ended up being an important part of the future. Not because I will it, but because people here have heard enough that there are others who can and do carry at least part of the banner themselves. That's what you need to have happen so that it's not just Dave Lawrence saying it, it's other people embracing it. How much I can't tell you, but we've clearly made some progress.

"What I am contemplating, urging, shoving, pushing is not some radical social experiment. It's not an ego trip; it is simply a sense of being fair. It is, after all, what this country is supposed to be about."[11]

David Lawrence's leadership, vision, and direction is enabling *The Miami Herald* to deal with Workforce 2000 issues. Through his vision and direction, the organization is making changes which will enable the newspaper to meet the challenges of the 21st Century. By using the five key sociotechnical elements, organizations can tailor plans like *The Miami Herald*'s to their specific needs. Organizational leaders providing vision to facilitate change will accelerate the process.

## 6. CHANGING ATTITUDES: THE SIGNIFICANT EMOTIONAL EVENT

When a commodity becomes scarce, users of that commodity respond with some type of emotional reaction. The response can even turn violent if the commodity is essential for survival. America's workforce demographics are changing at a time when organizations are downsizing or consolidating. Many jobs lost today will never return. The organizational myth and its by-products like "quotas" and "reverse discrimination" serve as fuel for the win-lose scenarios played daily as diverse groups are pitted against one another for the latest scarce resource, jobs. David Lawrence describes this dynamic extremely well:

"History generally interests me and my view of history is that you look back on all the great movements of humankind and every one of them was accompanied by enormous conflict. So I think often-times that doing what is right requires folks pushing and grating against one another. Now this clearly makes some folks uncomfortable, including people at this very newspaper who say, 'White guys don't have a chance anymore.' Now I say that's wrong — look around — white guys aren't exactly falling into the water out here. There are all sorts of examples of folks who are making it here who are white. In my view a white guy coming in here, who is brilliant, ought to be able to have a brilliant future. But simple mathematics will tell you that if the numbers remain constant and we need a more pluralistic staff

and management, then you are clearly going to have some dimin-
ished number of opportunities for folks who were in the majority
before. That is not the same, in my view, as 'I didn't get the job
because I am a white guy or whatever.' My experience is that
people need to find all sorts of reasons for why they haven't
succeeded. We all need to live with each other and ourselves.
When the question is, 'Why didn't I get that job?' an easy thing
to say is 'The system is rotten, they are only selecting 'these
kinds' of people.' One of the sad things that has happened in this
country, partly because of the Greedy Eighties, is that nobody
feels his or her job is safe anymore. No one is immune from it and
here at *The Miami Herald* we are a business that depends on
75% of our revenues from advertising. Our situation may be
different from other businesses because there is a particular
urgency about making sure that we have a diverse staff if we ever
hope to reach folks generally."[12]

Lawrence recognizes that *The Miami Herald*'s survival is
based on reaching markets dramatically affected by shifting demographics. He is also aware of the emotional conflict over jobs at
*The Miami Herald* that adjustment to a more diverse staff exacer-
bates. His comments on this issue offer some important clues why
much of today's diversity training will never lead to change. Too
often such training is directed at supplying general information to
groups already overloaded with rhetoric and opinions on the subject. Beneath the surface, strong emotions bubble about the multiple goals of diversity, downsizing, and financial success, but
those feelings are not allowed to surface in polite conversation.
Dysfunctional organizations have the added problem of negative
behavioral characteristics impeding any type of diversity discussion which could lead to change. The negative organizational
myth allows dysfunctional organizations to circumvent the entire
question because the myth says they are already practicing diversity. Erasing the negative organizational myth and its results will
only occur when individuals openly express and confront their
own emotional reactions. The knowledge acquired from the sociotechnical process provides a catalyst for substantive fact-based
discussion. Although this approach will not eliminate emotional
debate, it does reduce the intellectual value-based exchanges and
shifts the focus to the necessity for change.

In today's world, many organizations faced with the continuing challenges of a global society are finding that to be smaller, faster, and more flexible is the pathway to a successful future. These organizations find it is easier to create new entities than to attempt a breakdown of old paradigm thinking in the existing organizational environment. Such changes are not driven by social concerns or legal imperatives, but rather by the economic necessity to achieve a high level of productivity in an increasingly difficult and turbulent world marketplace.

Failures will occur even in these smaller organizations if older paradigm values continue to predominate. This is particularly true for dysfunctional organizations in which individuals are often averse to risk and will cling to the status quo unless forced to do otherwise. Some organizations recover from serious situations but most often hit rock bottom before change is possible. Morris Massey refers to this as a SEE (SIGNIFICANT EMOTIONAL EVENT).[13] The SEE becomes the reason to change. There are at least five areas of accelerating change that will become the SEEs of the next decade. They are the knowledge explosion, rapid product obsolescence, demographic shifts with the concomitant changing composition of the labor force, growing concern over personal and social issues, and the increasing internationalization of business. Throughout this book we have focused primarily on demographic shifts, but the second most influential SEE of the next decade will be the knowledge explosion. The knowledge explosion consists of workers more concerned about professional ethics and quality of service than organizational social status. It is comprised of a generation of individuals committed to their families and a balanced work and personal life. More knowledgeable and less malleable than the workers in the past, these people are the "pioneers" forging a pathway for new paradigm thinking.

This "movement" is already in progress; many of these knowledge workers have already started their own businesses and, in many instances, are competing with their former employers. Minorities and females determined to give diversity a chance comprise a major percentage of this group. Surrounding themselves with a diverse, knowledge-based staff, they are developing new organizations with a competitive advantage impossible under old paradigm rules.

CONCLUSION

Organizational knowledge gathered through historical assessment leads to solutions tailored to the organization's specific needs and provides opportunities for sustained improvement. By focusing on the interrelationships between the sociotechnical elements, management can move the organization beyond temporary solutions.

The primary emphasis in the effort to achieve quality in manufacturing today is oriented to processes. A similar focus on processes is needed to assimilate women, minorities, the disabled, and older workers into organizations to unleash the full potential of America's competitive Workforce 2000. Internal operating processes based on 1900 standards are anachronistic and incapable of yielding results needed for the future. When an organization's affirmative action efforts are narrowly concentrated on statistical information or awareness programs for the majority population, they are unlikely to produce any substantive changes. Although the gathering of statistics and sensitivity training are important, they are only the beginning of the change process, not the change itself. Dysfunctional groups benefit very little from this stage of change, especially if this information does not address the group's negative values. Transitioning to the new paradigm in dysfunctional organizations requires challenging behaviors and values which sustain exclusionary practices.

Reviewing the organization's strategy, structure, systems, and human resources (both people and systems) assists in identifying the elements that require change. That review and the subsequent changes leads to the formation of an overall system of decision-making that supports and encourages inclusion of all parts of the workforce. A strong commitment from Chief Executive Officers and senior level officials, like that of David Lawrence, brings leadership to the process. With vision and direction, managers can assure the organization's shift to a more diverse and fully qualified workforce. Through such efforts the "glass ceiling" and the negative organizational myth can become relics of the past.

# CHAPTER 6
## Conclusion

This book has identified the need for a new paradigm to assist organizations needing to change in order to assimilate Workforce 2000 individuals. Since World War II, American organizations have enjoyed worldwide economic dominance within the parameters of the old paradigm. Today, however, they can no longer depend on past successes for future economic leadership. For several years, journals, books, and newspapers have documented the necessity for change; yet it still goes unheeded by our leaders.

On the broader political, economic and social level, our country's leaders are responsible for facilitating a change process which will ensure America's future generations a role in the global society. The discussions that took place in October 1991 as Supreme Court nominee Clarence Thomas and Professor Anita Hill bared their souls for the world to see dramatized the urgent need for leaders who understand their new roles. The circus atmosphere surrounding that debate is symbolic of a society that has somehow traded the principles of fairness and justice for a system in which raw power and dysfunctional thinking rule. Across the country Americans eagerly participated in the search for truth and voiced their views about who was right and who was wrong.

Members of the congressional committee questioned the confirmation process. Women's groups, angered by the lack of concern for the gravity of sexual harassment, pointed angry fingers at the all-white male confirmation committee and took it to task for its insensitivity. At the same time, African-Americans cringed as racial stereotypes that many of them had fought for years to eliminate became the topic of every news and talk show and even over some breakfast tables. Yet, this debate was about much more than who was right. It also went far beyond male/female or racial issues. It was about the old paradigm and how it is ill-equipped to work in today's multicultural society. It was specifically about the time-worn statement uttered during any defense of old paradigm thinking: "It may not be the best process, but no one has found a better way." We will never be able to find a better way if we continue to use the same thinking that created the current system.

How was it possible during the Hill-Thomas debate for women's groups to rejoice at the exposure of the sexual harassment issue when African-Americans of both sexes were being subjected to analyses steeped in racial stereotypes? How could African-Americans cele-brate Anita Hill's bravery when the African-American male was being branded as a liar and sexual deviant for all the world to see? How could the African-American male defend the strength and intellect of Clarence Thomas while the reputation of a equally strong and intelligent African-American female was being destroyed? The key to those seeming enigmas is the process that leaves out signifi-cant portions of our society — a system that requires groups of people to look out for themselves because, if they do not, no one else will. We will never be able to repair that flawed process if the groups on the periphery of the current paradigm continue to simply add their point of view to the system. Such a solution is still singular thinking pushing against singular thinking. It can only result in a series of win-lose scenarios at a time when only plural solutions will assist America in maintaining a leadership position.

The Congressional committee in a fit of pique questioned the confirmation process which allowed someone in their ranks inten-tionally to leak a confidential report. The larger issue that needed to be addressed is our system's inability to find solutions to today's and tomorrow's problems. That is the root of the problem. If the leaders of this country are so far removed from what is really going on, how can they possibly find a remedy?

The debate over Hill and Thomas was occurring at the same time drugs were taking the lives of our children, thousands of people were homeless and hungry, the school system was graduating young adults who cannot read or write and the elderly and disabled were forgotten segments of our society. Perhaps our leadership is equally unaware of the reality of these issues. In the end, it does not matter who leaked what or who sold out to whom, who lied and who told the truth, because in the eyes of the rest of the world everyone involved symbolized America, and all Americans were the losers.

This debate began in earnest in the 1960s when sensible Americans came to realize that our society had to change patterns of behavior that had prevailed for centuries. At that time, some visionary organizational leaders recognized that civil rights issues reached beyond social and moral responsibilities and even over-shadowed legal compulsions. They understood that organizational survival, and ultimately that of our nation, rested on the incorpora-tion of groups previously excluded from the mainstream of society. Those leaders began to develop rational plans of investment in human capital within their organizations, the one type of capital that sets our country and its organizations apart from world competitors. They are now one step ahead of the game.

In contrast, today's old paradigm organizations are faced with increasingly difficult choices as we race toward the 21st century. The spectre of a more diverse workforce has once again unleashed latent tensions in American society and organizations. These ten-sions can reinforce the managerial tendency to "circle the wagons," and ignore environmental changes signaling a shift to a new para-digm. Yet, if these organizations do not change, they face increasing dangers in a turbulent national and world marketplace.

An understanding of the historical origins of their unique organizational personalities and concomitant value constructs can play an important role in these organizations and their response to change. Utilization of the sociotechnical process can enable them to uncover historical imprinting on their internal structures and sys-tems which affect organizational decision-making. Knowledge gathered during this process can lead to solutions tailored to the needs of their organization.

A healthy response to change also includes a careful examina-tion of organizational values. This examination will reveal impor-tant clues as to fairness and equity values which will enable organizations to incorporate individuals and groups not heard from in the past. On the other hand, dysfunctional organizations will have an extremely difficult time recognizing values and processes that reinforce exclusionary behavior. Even when confronted with the truth, such organizations will see only what they choose to see. Yet, they must recognize their unhealthy behavior before they can even begin a change process. Only through such recognition will they find it possible to take the first steps to removal of barriers like the "glass ceiling" encountered by individuals and groups comprising Workforce 2000. One important clue to spotting systemic problems in these organizations is the existence of the negative organizational myth. Publicly the organization may proclaim to the world its support for multicultural and diversity objectives when in reality its policies and procedures are calculated to subvert goals of fairness, equity and pluralism.

THE FUTURE

When asked about the Civil Rights Bill of 1991 and its importance to America, David Lawrence replied, "I don't even think about it. I'm not telling you that it's not important, I'm simply saying that the real pressure in this country needs to be put on the heads of institutions to do what is right. One institutional leader is the President of the United States. Other such leaders are the CEO's of our major institutions. They might be heads of newspapers, television stations, universities, businesses, etc. These are the folks you've got to get to. It can't bubble up from the bottom."[1]

Today and in the future, organizational leaders bear primary responsibility for creating an inclusionary environment linking all groups in American society to the mainstream. A secondary responsibility will be the maintenance of excellence standards while change takes place. These leaders must be capable of recognizing group norms which increase rather than decrease overall organizational performance. In the process of identifying group beliefs and translating them into organizational values, these leaders must be willing to place these values under a magnifying glass and to answer the new paradigm question: "How will these values affect our ability to make decisions utilizing individuals who do not look, think, or act exactly like us? The answer to this question will lead to solutions capable of catapulting today's organizations into a more successful future. The future is "Everybody's Business" and we must all take an active role in its development. For example, entrepreneurs in the start-up phase of their new businesses can articulate their workplace values and compare them to those required to address the new paradigm question. This will ensure that their structures and processes will accommodate differences, not similarities. Individuals not in leadership positions can assist change by voting for leaders aware of the necessity for change and willing to make decisions congruent with their awareness.

Many of the rules and regulations we live by today reflect the obsolete social values of a bygone era. Leadership from the top will enable our organizations to make changes needed for the 21st century. The more values brought to the organization, the more solutions it can generate to solve problems, and the more creative and innovative will be the answers. It is that innovation and creativity that will lead us to a more successful future.

# NOTES

## Chapter 1

1. Joel A. Barker, *Discovering the Future, the Business of Paradigms* (Lake Elmo, Minnesota: ILI Press, 1985), pp. 14–27.
2. Alvin Toffler, *The Third Wave* (New York: Bantam Books, 1981), pp. 61–62.
3. Rosabeth Kanter, *Men and Women of the Corporation* (New York: Basic Books, Inc., 1977), p. 20.
4. Hudson Institute, *Opportunity 2000: Creative Affirmative Action Strategies for a Changing Workforce* (Washington, D.C.: U.S. Department of Labor, 1988).
5. *Ibid.*, pp. 2–14.
6. Kanter, *op. cit.*, pp. 22–23.
7. Patrick E. Connor, *Organizations: Theory and Design* (Chicago: SRA, 1980), p. 20.
8. Kanter, *op. cit.*, p. 24.
9. William G. Scott & David K. Hart, *Organizational America* as cited in Scott, *et al, Organizational Theory: A Structural and Behavioral Analysis* (Homewood, Illinois: Richard D. Irwin, Inc., 1981), pp. 333–336.
10. Barker, *op. cit.*, p. 90.
11. Morris E. Massey, *The People Puzzle* (Old Tappan, New Jersey: Reston Publishing Co., Inc., 1979), pp. 8–23.

## Chapter 2

1. June Webb-Vignery, *Jacome's Department Store: Business and Culture in Tucson, Arizona, 1896–1980* (New York: Garland Publications, Inc., 1989).

2. Massey, *op. cit.*, pp. 8–23.
3. "By permission. From Webster's Ninth New Collegiate Dictionary © 1991 by Merriam-Webster Inc., publisher of the Merriam-
   Webster® dictionaries."
4. Massey, *op. cit.*, pp. 8–23.
5. Bart Ziegler, "Employee Inertia: Inept management is often to
   blame," *The Arizona Daily Star*, June 9, 1991, pp. 1, 6 G.
6. *Ibid.*
7. Barker, *op. cit.*, p. 90.
8. Morris, Massey, "What You Are Is" videotape participant's
   workbook (California: CBS Fox Co., 1984) p. 21.

## Chapter 3

1. Anne Wilson Schaef and Diane Fassel, *The Addictive Organization* (San Francisco: Harper & Row, 1988), pp. 60, 113, 123.
2. David Lawrence, "Pluralism," Knight-Ridder Management Conference, February 28, 1990.
3. Schaef & Fassel, *op. cit.*, p. 170.
4. *Ibid.*
5. *Ibid.*, pp. 113, 123.
6. *Ibid.*, pp. 62. 151.
7. *Ibid.*, pp. 60, 146.
8. For a discussion of repressive management strategies see: Robert H. Miles, *Macro Organizational Behavior* (Santa Monica,
   California: Goodyear Publishing Co., Inc., 1980), pp. 125–126.
9. David Lawrence Interview, July 23, 1991.
10. *Ibid.*
11. Schaef & Fassel, *op. cit.*, pp. 63–64, 87, 139–141, 152–153.
12. *Ibid.*, p. 182.
13. David Lawrence Interview, July 23, 1991.
14. Schaef & Fassel, *op. cit.*, pp. 158–160.
15. R. Roosevelt Thomas, Jr., *Beyond Race and Gender* (New York:
    Amacon, 1991), p. 21.
16. David Lawrence Interview, July 23, 1991.
17. Schaef & Fassel, *op. cit.*, pp. 83, 94.
18. *Ibid.*, p. 169.
19. *Ibid.*, p. 172.
20. *Ibid.*, p. 169.
21. *Ibid.*
22. *Ibid.*, pp. 164–176.

23. *Ibid.*, pp. 161, 169.
24. *Ibid.*, pp. 62–64, 151–156.
25. *Ibid.*, p. 125.
26. *Ibid.*, 134.
27. *Ibid.*, p. 202.
28. Paul Hersey and Kenneth H. Blanchard, *Management of Organizational Behavior: Utilizing Human Resources* (Englewood Cliffs, New Jersey: Prentice-Hall, Inc., 1982), pp. 2, 272.

## Chapter 4

1. *The Arizona Daily Star*, "Labor secretary swings hammer at 'glass ceiling'," August 9, 1991, p. 9 C.
2. U. S. Department of Labor, "A Report on the Glass Ceiling Initiative," (Washington, D.C.: U.S. Government Printing Office, 1991), pp. 13–17.
3. *Ibid.*
4. *The Arizona Daily Star*, Friday, August 9, 1991, p. 9 C.
5. Joseph Raelin, *Clash of Cultures, Managers Managing Professionals* (Boston: Harvard Business School Press, 1991) pp. 24, 25, 44–81.
6. Bill Platt, *¿Only English? Law and Language Policy in the United States* (Albuquerque: University of New Mexico Press, 1990), pp. 3–30.
7. Roseann Duenas Gonzalez & Paul Wong, The Cota-Ralls Study: An Investigation into the use of Spanish Speaking Employees of the Tucson Police Department (Unpublished study, December 10, 1990), Passim.
8. *The Arizona Daily Star*, July 3, 1991, p. 3 B.
9. Charles T. Maxey, Report on the Impact of the Use of Spanish Language Skills on the terms and conditions of Employment of Hispanic Personnel with the Tucson Police Department, City of Tucson (Unpublished study, December, 1990), pp. 32–35.
10. Federico Sanchez, Co-Chair, El Concilio letter to the Honorable Thomas Volgy, Mayor of the City of Tucson, July 16, 1991; *The Arizona Daily Star*, June 4, 1991, p. 1 B; June 1, 1991, p. 2 B.
11. Herman Kogan & Rick Kogan, *Pharmacist to the Nation: A History of Walgreen Co.: America's Leading Drug Store Chain* (Chicago: R. R. Donnelley & Sons Co., 1989), p. 277.
12. *Ibid.*

13. C. R. Walgreen III & L. D. Jorndt memo to all Management, April 19, 1991.
14. *Walgreen World*, "El Mundo de Walgreens," Vol. 58, Number 2, March/April 1991, p. 1.
15. Walgreens District Manager Mort Grayam Interview, August 7, 1991.
16. Walgreens Group Manager for Employee Development Marilyn Steffel Interview, August 7, 1991.
17. Walgreens District Manager Mort Grayam Interview, August 7, 1991.
18. *Ibid.; Walgreen World*, "The Power of Volunteers," Vol. 56, Number 6 (November/December, 1989), p. 1.

## Chapter 5

1. "A Report on the Glass Ceiling Initiative," p. 2.
2. David R. Hampton, *et al, Organizational Behavior and the Practice of Management* (Chicago: Scott, Foresman & Co., 1978), pp. 126–127.
3. Kathy Vandell & Lauren Fishbein, "With Bias Toward None," *Outlook Magazine*, Vol. 84, No. 41 (October/November, 1990), p. 13.
4. Thomas S. Kuhn, *The Structure of Scientific Revolutions* (Chicago: University of Chicago Press, 1970), p. 47.
5. Keith David, *Behavior at Work, Human Relations and Organizational Behavior* (New York: McGraw Hill Book Co., 1972), pp. 166–167.
6. *Ibid.*, p. 167.
7. "A Report on the Glass Ceiling Initiative," p. 4.
8. Robert R. Rehder, "Japanese Transplants: In Search of a Balanced and Broader Perspective," *Columbia Journal of World Business*, (Winter 1989), p. 18.
9. *Ibid.*
10. David Lawrence Interview, July 23, 1991.
11. *Ibid.*
12. *Ibid.*
13. Massey, *op. cit.*, pp. 237–239.

## Chapter 6

1. David Lawrence Interview, July 23, 1991.

# Index

Classical approach, 28
Classical theory, 11, 19, 20, 22, 23
Closed organizations, 23, 26, 32, 37, 42
Collective ethic, 13
Collectivist mentality, 18
Colonial, 5, 6
Color, 26, 31, 47, 54
Communication systems, 20, 32, 39, 40,
    41, 48, 60, 66
Community, 13
Compensation system, 37, 52
Competition, 3, 8, 45, 59
Conflict, 36, 38, 39, 40, 41, 42, 47
Conformity, 6
Conspirators, 64
Control, 34, 41, 49
Corporation, 6
*Cota and Falls, et al v. City of Tucson*, 57
Create, 23, 74
Creating, 1, 2, 3, 9
Creativity, 3, 16, 18, 63, 81
Crisis, 19, 40, 41, 42, 46, 49
Cubans, 60
Cultural barriers, 9, 60
— diversity, 36
— myth, 9
Culture, 57
— organizational, 2, 3, 15, 16, 32, 41,
    44, 51, 52, 53, 54, 56

Davis, Keith, 66
Decisions, 20
Decision-makers, 16
Decision-making loop, 22
Decision processes, 27, 31, 45, 66, 76, 79
Defensive tactics, 39
Demographics, 25, 49, 60, 62, 67, 73,
    74, 75
Denial system, 36, 39, 45, 48, 49, 65
Department stores, 15
Department of Labor, 51, 52, 53
Dependent care, 9
Diagnostic model, 3
Dinosaurs, 45, 46, 47
Disabilities in Employment Act of 1990, 9
Disability, 12, 32, 57, 61
Disabled, 1, 6, 8, 28, 53, 59, 66, 76, 78
— hiring 9
— promotion, 9
— Viet Nam veterans, 25, 26
*Discovering the Future*, 27

Discrimination, 3, 6, 9, 11, 25, 26, 37, 40,
    41, 46, 49, 67
— cultural, 9
— disabled, 9
— economically disadvantaged, 9
— gender, 8
— immigrant, 9
— older worker, 9
Discriminatory conduct, 9, 33, 34, 59
— practices, 11
Disinformation, 21
Dispensability, 13
Distortions from the past, 39
Diverse
— groups, 73
— human resources, 38
— perspectives, 38
— populations, 9
— staff, 74
— workforce, 13, 23, 26, 33, 35, 47, 60,
    62, 66, 71, 79
Diversity, 23, 25, 34, 36, 37, 38, 39, 42,
    46, 49, 53, 64, 65, 66, 69, 71, 74, 75
— training, 74
"Diversity Now," 39
Downsizing, 73, 74
Drug store, 59
Due process, 37
*Dun's Business Month*, 60
Dysfunctional, 1
— behaviors, 25, 41, 42, 67
— organizations, 16, 25, 26, 29, 32, 33,
    34, 36, 40, 42, 43, 48, 49, 55, 56,
    65, 66, 67, 69, 74, 75, 76, 79
— organizational personalities, 21, 24,
    28, 53
— symptoms, 33, 37, 40

Economic leadership, 5
Education, 34–47, 65
EEOC Uniform Guidelines on Employee
    Selection Procedures, 12
Effectiveness, 11, 31, 36, 42, 45, 59
Efficiency, 5, 7, 11, 22, 61
Eighteenth century, 5
Elderly, 78
Embassy Homes, 8
Emotional, 12, 48, 73, 74
Emotionality, 13
Employment
— practices, 10, 34, 35

90

Jacome, Carlos, 15
*Jacome's Department Store:*
  *Business & Culture in Tucson, Arizona,*
  *1896–1980,* 15
Japanese, 67
Jenkins, Barbara, 53–57
Job descriptions, 27
  — interviews, 38
  — rejection, 18
  — specifications, 37, 58
Johnson, Lyndon B., 25
Jones, Mary, 43

Kanter, Rosabeth, 10
Kennedy, John F., 25
KKK, 71
Knowledge explosion, 75
Kuhn, Thomas, 27, 66

Labor Department, 51, 52, 53
Labor (American), 2, 6
  — market, 6
  — supply, 9
Language, 57, 58, 59
Lawrence, David, 33, 38, 40, 41, 70, 71,
  72, 73, 74, 76, 80
Leaders, 66, 73, 77, 78, 80
Leadership, 20, 41, 42, 45, 48, 63, 64, 65,
  66, 69, 70, 71, 76, 77, 78, 81
Legal imperatives, 75
Liberal, 70, 71
Listens, 9
"Loser's Syndrome," 49, 56, 66, 69, 70
Loss of memory, 37
Louisiana, 61

Males, 7, 8, 10, 65, 78
Mainstream, 9, 79, 80
Malleability, 6, 13, 18
Managers, 7, 20, 25
Managerial, 10, 22
Management, 10, 38, 66
Manipulation, 34, 39, 44, 49, 65
Marketplace, 6, 25, 75
Martin, Lynn, 51, 53
Martinez, Richard, 58
Massey, Morris, 75
Mass-produced housing, 8
Media, 39
*Men and Women of the Corporation,* 10
Mental blocks, 23, 27
Mexicans, 60

Mexican-American Police Officers'
  Association, 57
Miami, Florida 60
Minorities, 14, 25, 26, 27, 42, 51, 52, 53,
  65, 66, 67, 72, 75, 76
Misinformation, 39
Monolingualism, 57, 58
"Moving finish line," 55
Moral, 11, 13, 14, 36, 44, 45, 79
Multicultural, 36, 64, 65, 78
Myth
  — organizational, 36, 63, 64, 65, 73,
    74, 76
  — social, 53, 63, 64

National origin, 26
Nativist, 57
Negative organizational myth, 64, 65
New England factory system, 10
"new" workforce, 1, 2, 6, 8, 9
1960s, 2, 5, 8, 79
1991 Civil Rights Act, 5, 25, 27
Nineteenth Century, 5, 6
Nixon Presidency, 44
Nondiscrimination, 25, 26, 31, 33, 42

Obedience, 6, 13
Obstacles, 6, 9, 28
  — social, 10
Office of Federal Contract Compliance
  Programs (OFCCP), 35
"Old boy network," 19
Older workers, 1, 6, 8, 28, 31, 53, 59, 76
  — barriers to employment, 9
Organizations
  — American, 14
  — dysfunctional, 16, 25, 26, 29, 32, 33,
    34, 36, 40, 42, 43, 48, 49, 55, 56,
    64, 65, 66, 67, 69, 74, 75, 79
  — healthy, 16, 19, 36, 39, 47, 66, 70, 79
  — modern, 2, 7, 8, 10, 11, 13, 14, 66
Organizational
  — American, 6, 9
  — barriers, 1, 9, 10, 11, 33, 35, 67, 80
  — behavior, 2, 3, 42, 49
  — business sectors, 51
  — change, 3, 41, 42, 49, 63
  — climate, 26
  — code, 13
  — control, 7, 43
  — culture, 2, 3, 15, 16, 32, 41, 44, 51,
    52, 53, 54, 56